Contents

DUDLEY

Welcome to Coaching

Coaching young people is an exciting way to be involved in sport. But it isn't easy. Some coaches are overwhelmed by the responsibilities involved in helping players through their early sport experiences. And that's not surprising, because coaching youngsters requires more than bringing the balls to the field and letting them play. It also involves preparing them physically and mentally to compete effectively, fairly, and safely in their sport and providing them with a positive role model.

This book will help you meet the challenges and experience the many rewards of coaching young players. You'll learn how to meet your responsibilities as a coach, communicate well, provide for safety, and teach tactics and skills in a fun way. You'll also learn strategies for coaching on game day. Over 30 activities are included throughout the text and in one of the book's appendixes, to help you with your practices. We also provide sample practice plans and season plans to guide you through your season.

This book serves as a text for ASEP's Coaching Youth Soccer course. If you would like more information about this course or other American Sport Education Program courses and resources, please contact us at the following address:

ASEP
P.O. Box 5076
Champaign, IL 61825-5076
800-747-5698
www.ASEP.com

Welcome From US Youth Soccer

Dear Coach:

On behalf of US Youth Soccer, welcome to *Coaching Youth Soccer*. It is one of many resources available to you through the American Sport Education Program (ASEP) and US Youth Soccer. Whether it's learning how to teach proper fundamental skills or how to communicate better, this book can guide you through your experience of coaching youth soccer.

Here you will find fresh ideas on how to coach children. They may be different from the way you were coached, but these methods are best for grooming passionate players. You will find activities and plenty of resources to aid you in your coaching journey. These coaching methods are based on our experiences in teaching the 300,000 coaches of US Youth Soccer across the USA.

You have at your fingertips a book full of ideas to get you through your first season and many more to come. You will find it easy to follow, an excellent introduction to coaching youth. Between ASEP and US Youth Soccer you will have access to a wealth of practical information on coaching.

Your coaching will have a profound impact on the players you influence, for today and many years to come. On behalf of the players, thank you for coaching youth soccer!

Keep kicking,

Sam Snow
Director of Coaching Education

Activities Finder

	Activity title	Related age group	Page
Offensive technical skills			
Dribbling	Dribbling Touch	U6, U8, U10, U12, U14	Page 68
	Dribble Attack	U6, U8, U10, U12, U14	Page 151
	Four-Goal Mayhem	U8, U10, U12, U14	Page 152
Passing	Tiger Ball	U6, U8, U10, U12, U14	Page 70
	Kicking for Distance	U8, U10, U12, U14	Page 72
	Short and Sharp	U8, U10, U12, U14	Page 153
	The Long Bomb	U6, U8, U10, U12, U14	Page 154
Receiving	Horseshoes	U6, U8, U10, U12, U14	Page 75
	Thighs	U10, U12, U14	Page 77
	Windows	U6, U8, U10, U12, U14	Page 78
	Hot Potato	U6, U8, U10, U12, U14	Page 158
Heading	Head Start	U12, U14	Page 80
	Heads Up	U12, U14	Page 155
Shooting	Hot Shots	U6, U8, U10, U12, U14	Page 82
	Strike Force	U6, U8, U10, U12, U14	Page 156
	Shooting Stars	U6, U8, U10, U12, U14	Page 157
Defensive technical skills			
Marking	Marking Man	U8, U10, U12, U14	Page 89
	Monkey On Their Backs	U6, U8, U10, U12, U14	Page 161
Tackling	Double Zone	U8, U10, U12, U14	Page 93
	The Duel	U6, U8, U10, U12, U14	Page 162
	Crunch Time	U6, U8, U10, U12, U14	Page 163
Intercepting passes	Interception	U6, U8, U10, U12, U14	Page 95
Making clearances	Neutral Zone	U8, U10, U12, U14	Page 96
Goalkeeping	Narrow Enough	U10, U12, U14	Page 164
	Keeper Wars	U10, U12, U14	Page 165
	Bowling Balls	U6, U8, U10, U12, U14	Page 166
	On the Money	U6, U8, U10, U12, U14	Page 167
	Over the Top	U10, U12, U14	Page 168
	What's the Scoop	U10, U12, U14	Page 169
	Punting Contest	U10, U12, U14	Page 106

Key to Diagrams

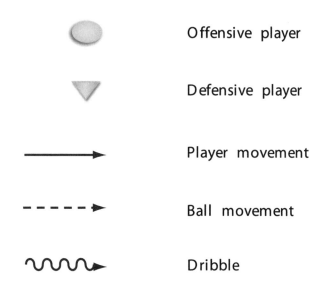

Offensive player

Defensive player

Player movement

Ball movement

Dribble

Stepping Into Coaching

I f you are like most youth soccer coaches, you have probably been recruited from the ranks of concerned parents, sport enthusiasts, or community volunteers. Like many rookie and veteran coaches, you probably have had little formal instruction on how to coach. But when the call went out for coaches to assist with the local youth soccer program, you answered because you like children and enjoy soccer and perhaps because you want to be involved in a worthwhile community activity.

Your initial coaching assignment may be difficult. Like many volunteers, you may not know everything there is to know about soccer or about how to work with children, especially of such varying ages. *Coaching Youth Soccer* will help you learn the basics of coaching soccer effectively. To begin with, we look at the responsibilities you have as a coach. We also talk about what to do when your child is on the team you coach. Finally, we examine five tools for being an effective coach.

Your Responsibilities As a Coach

Coaching at any level involves much more than designing set plays for free kicks or drawing up team formations. Coaching involves accepting the tremendous responsibility you face when parents put their children into your care. As a soccer coach, you'll be called on to do the following:

1. *Provide a safe physical environment.*

   Playing soccer holds inherent risks, but as a coach you're responsible for regularly inspecting the practice and game fields and the equipment (see Facilities and Equipment Checklist in appendix A on page 140). Reassure players and parents that, to avoid injury, they will learn the safest techniques and that you have an emergency action plan you will be following (see chapter 4 for more information).

2. *Communicate in a positive way.*

   As you can already see, you have a lot to communicate. You'll communicate not only with your players and parents but also with coaching staff, officials, administrators, and others. Communicate in a positive way that demonstrates you have the best interests of the players at heart (see chapter 2 for more information).

3. *Teach the fundamental skills of soccer.*

   When teaching the fundamental skills of soccer, keep in mind that soccer is a game; you want to be sure that your players have fun. Therefore, we ask that you help all players be the best they can be by creating a fun, yet productive, practice environment. To help you do so, we'll show you an innovative games approach to teaching and practicing the tactics and skills young players need to know—an approach that kids thoroughly enjoy (see chapter 5 for more information). Additionally, to help your players improve their skills, you need to have a sound understanding of offensive and defensive skills (see chapters 7 and 8).

4. *Teach the rules of soccer.*

   Introduce the rules of soccer and incorporate them into individual instruction (see chapter 3). You can teach many rules in the first practice, during the course of gamelike activities and small-sided games. Plan to review the rules, however, any time an opportunity naturally arises in practices.

5. *Direct players in competition.*

   Game direction includes determining starting lineups and a substitution plan, relating appropriately to officials and to opposing coaches and players, and making sound tactical decisions during games (see chapter 9 for more information on coaching during games). Remember that the focus is not on winning at all costs, but on coaching your kids to compete well, do their best, improve their soccer skills, and strive to win within the rules.

6. *Help your players become fit and value fitness for a lifetime.*

   We want young players to become fit so that they can play soccer safely and successfully. We also want them to understand the value of fitness, learn to become fit on their own, and enjoy training. Thus, we ask you not to make them do push-ups or run laps for punishment. Make it fun to get fit for soccer, and make it fun to play the game so that they'll stay fit for a lifetime.

7. *Help young people develop character.*

   Character development includes learning, caring, being honest and respectful, and taking responsibility. These intangible qualities are no less important to teach than the skill of dribbling well. We ask you to teach these values to players by demonstrating and encouraging behaviors that express these values at all times. For example, in dribbling, stress to young players the importance of learning when and where to dribble, helping their teammates, playing within the rules, and showing respect for their opponents. Help them understand that they are responsible for winning the individual battle on every play, even though they may not be recognized individually for their efforts.

As you exercise your responsibilities, remember that every player is an individual. You must provide a wholesome environment in which each one has the opportunity to learn how to play the game without fear while having fun and enjoying the overall soccer experience.

Coaching Your Own Child

Coaching can become even more complicated when your child plays on the team you coach. Many coaches are parents, but the two roles should not be confused. As a parent, you are responsible only for yourself and your child, but as a coach you are also responsible for the organization, all the players on the team, and their parents. Because of this additional responsibility your behavior on the soccer field will be different from your behavior at home, and your son or daughter may not understand why.

Coaching Tip

Some parents have found that coaching helps keep their own children involved in soccer. Others find coaching their own children a recipe for disaster, because the child resents the switch from nurturing parent to neutral or demanding coach who can't play favorites. Discuss the decision with your child.

For example, imagine the confusion of a young boy who is the center of his parents' attention at home but is barely noticed by his father (who is the coach) in the sport setting. Or consider the mixed signals a young girl receives when her skill is constantly evaluated by her mother, the coach, who otherwise rarely comments on her daughter's activities. You need to explain to your child what your new responsibilities are and how they will affect your relationship when you're coaching. Take the following steps to avoid problems in coaching your own child:

- Ask your child whether she wants you to coach the team.
- Explain why you want to be involved with the team.
- Discuss with your child how your interactions will change when you take on the role of coach at practices or games.
- Limit your coaching behavior to when you are in the coaching role.
- Avoid parenting during practice or game situations, in order to keep your role clear in your child's mind.
- Reaffirm your love for your child, irrespective of his performance on the soccer field.

Five Tools of an Effective Coach

Have you purchased the traditional coaching tools—things like disc cones, coaching clothes, sport shoes, and a water bottle? They'll help you in the act of coaching, but to be successful you'll need five other tools that you cannot buy. These tools are available only through self-examination and hard work; they're easy to remember with the acronym COACH:

C   Comprehension

O   Outlook

A   Affection

C   Character

H   Humor

Comprehension

Coaching requires that you comprehend the rules and skills of soccer. You must understand the basic elements of the sport. To improve your comprehension of soccer, take the following steps:

- Read about the rules of soccer in chapter 3 of this book.
- Read about the fundamental skills of soccer in chapters 7 and 8.
- Read additional soccer coaching books, including those available from the American Sport Education Program (ASEP).
- Contact youth soccer organizations, including US Youth Soccer (www.usyouthsoccer.org).
- Attend soccer coaching clinics.
- Talk with more experienced coaches.
- Observe local college, high school, and youth soccer games.
- Watch soccer games on television.

In addition to having soccer knowledge, you must implement proper training and safety methods so that your players can participate with little risk of injury. Even then, injuries may occur. More often than not, you'll be the first person responding to your players' injuries, so be sure you understand the basic emergency care procedures described in chapter 4. Also, read in that chapter how to handle more serious sport injury situations.

Outlook

This coaching tool refers to your perspective and goals—what you seek as a coach. The most common coaching objectives are to (a) have fun; (b) help players develop their physical, mental, and social skills; and (c) help players strive to play their best consistently. Thus, your outlook involves your priorities, your planning, and your vision for the future. See Assessing Your Priorities to learn more about the priorities you set for yourself as a coach.

Assessing Your Priorities

Even though all coaches focus on competition, we want you to focus on *positive* competition. Keep the pursuit of victory in perspective—make decisions that first, are in the best interest of the players, and second, will help to win the match.

How do you know whether your outlook and priorities are in order? Here's a little test:

1. Which situation would you be most proud of?
    a. *Knowing that each participant enjoyed playing soccer.*
    b. *Seeing that all players improved their soccer skills.*
    c. *Winning the league championship.*

2. Which statement best reflects your thoughts about sport?
    a. *If it isn't fun, don't do it.*
    b. *Everyone should learn something every day.*
    c. *Sport isn't fun if you don't win.*

3. How would you like your players to remember you?
    a. *As a coach who was fun to play for.*
    b. *As a coach who provided a good base of fundamental skills.*
    c. *As a coach who had a winning record.*

4. Which would you most like to hear a parent of a player on your team say?
    a. *Mike really had a good time playing soccer this year.*
    b. *Nicole learned some important lessons playing soccer this year.*
    c. *Willie played on the first-place soccer team this year.*

5. Which of the following would be the most rewarding moment of your season?
    a. *Having your team want to continue playing, even after practice is over.*
    b. *Seeing one of your players finally master the skill of dribbling.*
    c. *Winning the league championship.*

Look over your answers. If you most often selected "*a*" responses, then having fun is most important to you. A majority of "*b*" answers suggests that skill development is what attracts you to coaching. And if "*c*" was your most frequent response, winning is tops on your list of coaching priorities. If your priorities are in order, your players' well-being will take precedence over your team's win-loss record every time.

ASEP has a motto that will help you keep your outlook in line with the best interests of the kids on your team. It summarizes in four words all you need to remember when establishing your coaching priorities:

Athletes First, Winning Second

This motto recognizes that striving to win is an important, even vital, part of sports. But it emphatically states that no efforts to win should be made at the expense of the player's well-being, development, and enjoyment. Take the following actions to better define your outlook:

- With your coaches, determine your priorities for the season.
- Prepare for situations that challenge your priorities.
- Set goals for yourself and your players that are consistent with your priorities.
- Plan how you and your players can best attain your goals.
- Review your goals frequently to be sure that you are staying on track.

Affection

Another vital tool you need in your coaching kit is a genuine concern for the young people you coach. It requires having a passion for kids, a desire to share with them your enjoyment and knowledge of soccer, and the patience and understanding that allow each player to grow from being involved in sport. You can demonstrate your affection and patience in many ways, including the following:

- Make an effort to get to know each player on your team.
- Treat each player as an individual.
- Empathize with players trying to learn new and difficult skills.
- Treat players as you would like to be treated under similar circumstances.
- Control your emotions.
- Show your enthusiasm for being involved with your team.
- Keep an upbeat tempo and a positive tone in all of your communications.

Character

The fact that you have decided to coach young soccer players probably means that you think participation in sport is important. But whether or not such participation develops character in your players depends as much on you as it does on the sport itself. How can you help your players build character?

Having good character means modeling appropriate behaviors for sport and life. That means more than just saying the right things—what you say and what you do must match. There is no place in coaching for the "Do as I say, not as I do" philosophy. Challenge, support, encourage, and reward every youngster, and your players will be more likely to accept, even celebrate, their differences. Be in control before, during, and after all practices and games. And don't be afraid to admit that you were wrong. No one is perfect.

Each member of your coaching staff should consider the following steps to becoming a good role model:

- Take stock of your strengths and weaknesses.
- Build on your strengths.
- Set goals for yourself to improve on those areas you don't want to see copied.
- If you slip up, apologize to your team and to yourself. You'll do better next time.

Humor

Humor is an often overlooked coaching tool. For our purpose, it means having the ability to laugh at yourself and with your players during practices and contests. Nothing helps balance the seriousness of a skill session like a chuckle or two. And a sense of humor puts in perspective the many mistakes your players will make. So don't get upset over each miscue or respond negatively to erring players. Allow your players and yourself to enjoy the ups, and don't dwell on the downs. Here are some tips for injecting humor into your practices:

- Make practices fun by including a variety of activities.
- Keep all players involved in games and skill practices.
- Consider laughter by your players a sign of enjoyment, not of waning discipline.
- Smile!

2

Communicating
As a Coach

In chapter 1 you learned about the tools you need for coaching: comprehension, outlook, affection, character, and humor. These are essentials for effective coaching; without them, you'd have a difficult time getting started. But none of the tools will work if you don't know how to use them with your players—and doing so requires skillful communication. This chapter examines what communication is and how you can become a more effective communicator.

Coaches often mistakenly believe that communication occurs only when they're instructing players to do something, but verbal commands are only a small part of the communication process. More than half of what you communicate is conveyed nonverbally. So remember when you are coaching: Actions speak louder than words.

Communication in its simplest form involves two people: a sender and a receiver. The sender transmits the message verbally, through facial expressions, and possibly through body language. Once the message is sent, the receiver must receive it and, optimally, understand it. A receiver who fails to pay attention or listen will miss part, if not all, of the message.

Sending Effective Messages

Young players often have little understanding of the rules and skills of soccer and probably even less confidence in their ability to play the game. So they need accurate, understandable, and supportive messages to help them along. That's why your verbal and nonverbal messages count.

Verbal Messages

"Sticks and stones may break my bones, but words will never hurt me" isn't true. Spoken words can have a strong and lasting effect. Coaches' words are particularly influential because youngsters place great importance on what coaches say. Perhaps you, like many former youth sport participants, have a difficult time remembering much of anything you were told by your elementary school teachers, but you can still recall several specific things your coaches at that level said to you. Such is the lasting effect of a coach's comments to a player.

Whether you are correcting misbehavior, teaching a player how to pass the ball, or praising a player for good effort, you should consider a number of things when sending a message verbally:

- Be positive and honest.
- State it clearly and simply.
- Say it loud enough, and say it again.
- Be consistent.

Be Positive and Honest

Nothing turns people off like hearing someone nag all the time, and players react similarly to a coach who gripes constantly. Kids particularly need encouragement because they often doubt their abilities to perform in a sport. Look for what your players do well and tell them. But don't cover up poor or incorrect play with rosy words of praise. Kids know all too well when they've erred, and no cheerfully expressed cliché can undo their mistakes. If you fail to acknowledge players' errors, they will think you are a phony.

An effective way to correct a performance error is to first point out the part of the skill that the player performed correctly. Then explain—in a positive manner—the error the player made and show her the correct way to do it. Finish by encouraging the player and emphasizing the correct performance.

Be sure not to follow a positive statement with the word *but*. For example, don't say, "That was good accuracy on your pass, Kelly, but if you follow through with your kick a little more, you'll get more zip on the ball." Such a remark causes many kids to ignore the positive statement and focus on the negative one. Try something like this: "That was good accuracy on your pass, Kelly. And if you follow through with your kick a little more, you'll get more zip on the ball. That was right on target. Way to go."

State It Clearly and Simply

Positive and honest messages are good, but only if expressed directly in words your players understand. Beating around the bush is ineffective and inefficient. And if you ramble, your players will miss the point of your message and probably lose interest. Here are tips for saying things clearly:

- Organize your thoughts before speaking to your players.
- Know your subject as completely as possible.
- Explain things thoroughly, but don't bore your players with long-winded monologues.
- Use language your players can understand and be consistent in your terminology. However, avoid trying to be hip by using their age group's slang.

Say It Loudly Enough, and Say It Again

Talk to your team in a voice that all members can hear. A crisp, vigorous voice commands attention and respect; garbled and weak speech is tuned out. It's OK, and in fact appropriate, to soften your voice when speaking to a player individually about a personal problem. But most of the time your messages will be for all your players to hear, so make sure they can. An enthusiastic voice also motivates players and tells them you enjoy being their coach. A word of caution, however: Avoid dominating the setting with a booming voice that distracts attention from players' performances.

Coaching Tip

Remember, terms that you are familiar with and understand may be completely foreign to your players, especially the beginners. Use a vocabulary appropriate to the age group. A 6-year-old most likely will not comprehend some words that a 12-year-old will understand.

Sometimes what you say, even if you state it loudly and clearly, won't sink in the first time. This may be particularly true when young players hear words they don't understand. To avoid boring repetition and still get your message across, say the same thing in a slightly different way. For instance, you might first tell your players, "Mark your opponents tighter!" If they don't appear to understand, you might say, "When your opponents are in scoring range, you can't give them the chance to shoot or pass the ball forward." The second form of the message may get through to players who missed it the first time around.

Be Consistent

People often say things in ways that imply a different message. For example, a touch of sarcasm added to the words "Way to go!" sends an entirely different message than the words themselves suggest. Avoid sending mixed messages. Keep the tone of your voice consistent with the words you use. And don't say something one day and contradict it the next; players will get their wires crossed.

Keep your terminology consistent. Many soccer terms describe the same or a similar skill. One coach may use the term *halfback* to describe a position in the middle of the team, whereas another coach may call the same position *midfielder*. Both are correct. To be consistent as a staff, however, agree on all terms before the start of the season and then stay with them.

Nonverbal Messages

Just as you must be consistent in the tone of voice and words you use, you must also keep your verbal and nonverbal messages consistent. An extreme example of failing to do so would be shaking your head, indicating disapproval, and at the same time telling a player, "Nice try." Which is the player to believe, your gesture or your words?

You can send messages nonverbally in several ways. Facial expressions and body language are just two of the more obvious forms of nonverbal signals that can help you when you coach. Keep in mind that a coach needs to be a teacher first, and any action that detracts from the message you are trying to convey should be avoided.

Facial Expressions

The look on a person's face is the quickest clue to what he thinks or feels. Your players know this, so they will study your face, looking for a sign that will tell them more than the words you say. Don't try to fool them by putting on a happy or blank mask. They'll see through it, and you'll lose credibility.

Serious, stone-faced expressions provide no cues to kids who want to know how they are performing. When faced with such, kids will just assume you're unhappy or disinterested. Don't be afraid to smile. A smile from a coach can give a great boost to an unsure player. Plus, a smile lets your players know that you are happy coaching them. But don't overdo it, or they won't be able to tell when you are genuinely pleased by something they've done and when you are just putting on a smiling face.

Body Language

What would your players think you were feeling if you came to practice slouched over with your head down and shoulders slumped? That you were tired, bored, or unhappy? What would they think you were feeling if you watched them during a contest with your hands on your hips, your jaws clenched, and your face reddened? That you were upset with them, disgusted at an official, or mad at a fan? Probably some or all of these things would enter your players' minds. None of them are impressions you want your players to have of you. That's why you should carry yourself in a pleasant, confident, and vigorous manner.

Physical contact can also be an essential use of body language. A handshake, a pat on the head, an arm around the shoulder, and even a big hug are effective ways to show approval, concern, affection, and joy to your players. Youngsters are especially in need of this type of nonverbal message. Keep within the obvious moral and legal limits, of course, but don't be reluctant to touch your players, sending a message that can only be expressed by such contact.

> **Coaching Tip**
> A good-humored, energetic posture not only projects happiness with your coaching role but also provides a good example for your young players who may model your behavior. Whereas prepubescent children do pick up on the coach's mannerisms, pubescent children are particularly aware of the coach's actions. Be prepared at all times to walk the talk.

Improving Your Receiving Skills

Now, let's examine the other half of the communication process: receiving messages. Too often, good senders are poor receivers of messages. As a coach of young players, you must be able to fulfill both roles effectively.

The requirements for receiving messages are quite simple, but some find receiving skills less satisfying than sending skills; therefore, they do not work at them. People seem to enjoy hearing themselves talk more than they enjoy hearing others talk. But if you learn the keys to receiving messages and make a strong effort to use them with your players, you'll be surprised by what you've been missing.

Pay Attention

First, you must pay attention—you must want to hear what others have to communicate to you. That's not always easy when you're busy coaching and have many things competing for your attention. But in one-on-one or team meetings with players, you must focus on what they are telling you, both verbally and nonverbally. You'll be amazed at the little signals you pick up. Focused attention not only helps you catch every word your players say but also helps you take in your players' moods and physical states. In addition, you'll get an idea of your players' feelings toward you and others on the team.

Listen Carefully

Perhaps more than anything else we do, how we receive messages from others demonstrates how much we care for the sender and for what that person has to tell us. If you have little regard for your players or for what they have to say, it will show in how you attend to them. Check yourself. Do you find your mind wandering to what you are going to do after practice, while one of your players is talking to you? Do you frequently have to ask your players, "What did you say?" If so, you need to work on the receiving mechanics of attending and listening. But perhaps the most critical question you should ask yourself, if you find that you're missing the messages your players send, is this: Do I care?

Providing Feedback

So far we've discussed the sending and receiving of messages separately. But we all know that senders and receivers switch roles several times during an interaction. One person initiates a communication by sending a message to another person, who receives the message. The receiver then becomes the sender by responding to the person who sent the initial message. These verbal and nonverbal responses are called feedback.

Your players will look to you for feedback all the time. They will want to know how you think they are performing, what you think of their ideas, and whether their efforts please you. You can respond in many different ways, and how you respond will strongly affect your players. They will react most favorably to positive feedback.

Praising players when they have performed or behaved well is an effective way of encouraging them to repeat (or try to repeat) that behavior. And positive feedback for effort is an especially effective way to motivate youngsters to work on difficult skills. Rather than shouting at players who have made mistakes and giving them negative feedback, try offering positive feedback by letting them know what they did correctly and how they can improve. Sometimes just the way you word feedback can make it more encouraging than not. For example, instead of saying, "Don't shoot the ball that way," you might say, "Shoot the ball this way." Then your players will focus on what to do instead of what not to do.

Positive feedback can be verbal or nonverbal. Telling young players that they have performed well, especially in front of teammates, is a great way to boost their confidence. And a pat on the back or a handshake communicates that you recognize a player's performance.

Communicating With Others

Coaching involves not only sending and receiving messages and providing proper feedback to players but also interacting with members of the staff, parents, fans, officials, and opposing coaches. If you don't communicate effectively with these groups, your coaching career will be unpleasant and short lived. Try the following suggestions for communicating with these groups.

Coaching Staff

Before you hold your first practice, the coaching staff must meet and discuss the roles and responsibilities that each coach will undertake during the year. Staff responsibilities can be divided into head coach, assistant coaches, and team manager, depending on the number of volunteers. Some clubs may also have a goalkeeper coach. The head coach has the final responsibility for all phases of the game, but the assistant coaches should take as much responsibility for their roles as possible.

Before practices start, the coaching staff must also discuss and agree on terminology, plans for practice, organization on game day, and methods of communicating during practices and games. The coaches on your staff must present a united front; they must all take a similar approach to coaching, interacting with players and parents, and interacting with one another. Conduct discussions of disagreements away from the playing field so that each coach can have a say and the staff can come to an agreement.

Parents

A player's parents need to be assured that their child is under the direction of a coach who is both knowledgeable about the sport and concerned about each youngster's well-being. You can put their worries to rest by holding a preseason orientation meeting for parents, in which you describe your background and your approach to coaching (see Preseason Meeting Topics).

If parents contact you with a concern during the season, listen to them closely and try to offer positive responses. If you need to communicate with parents, catch them after a practice, give them a phone call, or send a note through e-mail or the U.S. mail. Messages sent to parents through players are too often lost, misinterpreted, or forgotten. Parents may also connect with US Youth Soccer's parent assistance program located at www.usyouthsoccer.org.

Preseason Meeting Topics

1. Share your philosophy of coaching.

2. Outline paperwork that is needed for the club:
   - Copy of player's birth certificate
   - Completed player's application and payment record
   - Participation agreement form
   - Informed consent form
   - Emergency information card

3. Review the inherent risks of soccer and other safety issues and go over your emergency action plan.

4. Inform parents of uniform and equipment costs and needs.

5. Review the season practice schedule including date, location, and time of each practice.

6. Discuss nutrition, hydration, and rest for players.

7. Explain goals for the team.

8. Cover methods of communication: e-mail list, emergency phone numbers, interactive Web site, and so on.

9. Discuss ways that parents can help with the team.

10. Discuss standards of conduct for coaches, players, and parents.

11. Provide time for questions and answers.

Fans

The stands probably won't be overflowing at your matches, which means that you'll more easily hear the few fans who criticize your coaching. When you hear something negative about the job you're doing, don't respond. Keep calm, consider whether the message had any value, and if not, forget it. Acknowledging critical, unwarranted comments from a fan during a match will only encourage others to voice their opinions. So put away your rabbit ears, and communicate to fans, through your actions, that you are a confident, competent coach.

Prepare your players, too, for fans' criticisms. Tell them it is you, not the spectators, they should listen to. If you notice that one of your players is rattled by a fan's comment, reassure the player that your evaluation is more objective and favorable—and it's the one that counts.

Officials

How you communicate with officials will have a great influence on the way your players behave toward them; therefore, you must set an example. Greet officials with a handshake, an introduction, and perhaps casual conversation about the upcoming match. Indicate your respect for them before, during, and after the game. Don't make nasty remarks, shout, or use disrespectful body gestures. Your players will see you do these things, and they'll get the idea that such behavior is appropriate. Plus, if the official hears or sees you, the communication between the two of you will break down.

Opposing Coaches

Make an effort to visit with the coach of the opposing team before the game. During the game, don't get into a personal feud with the opposing coach. Remember—it's the kids, not the coaches, who are competing. And by getting along well with the opposing coach, you'll show your players that competition involves cooperation.

3

Understanding Rules and Equipment

Soccer is a simple game played by teams divided into 3 to 11 players per side. It is governed by rules that are modified for the age group that you are coaching. This introduction to the basic rules of soccer won't cover every rule of the game but will give you the fundamentals for working with players who are 6 to 14 years old. This chapter covers field markings, ball and goal sizes, and equipment. It also describes player positions, game procedures, and scoring; reviews the rules of play; and gives an overview of officiating and common officiating signals.

Age Modifications for Soccer

Before we begin, however, familiarize yourself with the concept of adjusting the size of the field, goal, and ball; the number of players on the field; and the duration of the game for various age groups to accommodate players' developmental and skill levels. These adjustments are as follows:

	U6	U8	U10	U12	U14
Players on team	Single field method: 4-6 Dual field method: 8-10	Single field method: 6-8 Dual field method: 10-12	Single field method: 9-11 Dual field method: 14-16	11-13	11-18
Ball size	3	3	4	4	5
Goal size	6 × 18 ft or smaller	6 × 18 ft or smaller	6 × 18 ft	6 × 18 ft	8 × 24 ft
Field size	30 × 25 yd	35 × 30 yd	60 × 45 yd	80 × 55 yd	105 × 65 yd
Players on field	3 per team	4 per team	6 per team	8 per team	11 per team
Length of game	4 × 8 min	4 × 12 min	2 × 25 min	2 × 30 min	2 × 35 min

For more detailed information on rules modifications, please refer to the US Youth Soccer playing recommendations for each specific age group at www.usyouthsoccer.org.

Field

The Laws of the Game allow for the length and width of the field to vary, within set yardages, for every age group and level of competition. The field markings within the boundary lines must be the same for every level of competition, as shown in figure 3.1, but they are modified for the specific age groups. Some field markings that you will see on the field of play for teenage and adult soccer fields will not be on the field for the younger players. For example, on the U6 and U8 fields of play the penalty area is not marked on the field as it is for the U10 and older age groups. The following markings define all fields (for additional soccer terms, please refer to appendix B on page 145):

- *Goal:* The area into which players try to shoot the ball to score points. A goal sits in the middle of the goal line at each end of the playing field but extends past the field itself. It is marked by two goalposts, a crossbar, and netting.
- *Goal line:* The end line of the field, on which the goal sits. The goal line runs from corner to corner.
- *Touchline:* The sideline that runs the length of the field of play from corner to corner.
- *Corner arc:* The four one-yard arcs, one in each corner of the field of play, from which players take corner kicks.
- *Goal area:* The small box immediately in front of the goal from which players take the goal kick.
- *Penalty kick spot:* The spot inside the penalty area from which players take penalty kicks.
- *Penalty area:* The large box in front of the goal. Fouls committed by the defending team that normally result in a direct free kick will result in a penalty kick when the foul is committed inside the penalty area. This is the area in which the goalkeeper may use his hands.
- *Penalty arc:* An arc drawn outside the penalty area, at a radius similar to the one for the center circle, from the penalty spot. No players are allowed within this arc when a penalty kick is being taken.
- *Halfway line:* The line that runs across the field of play from touchline to touchline and divides the field in half.

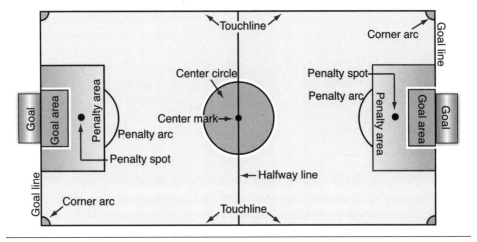

Figure 3.1   Soccer field markings.

- *Center circle:* The circle in the center of the field surrounding the center mark outside of which the defending team must remain until the ball is put into play at a kickoff.
- *Center mark:* The spot on the halfway line where the ball is placed for a kickoff.

Player Equipment

Soccer players need very little equipment to play the game. These items include multistudded soccer shoes (recommended for outdoor play but not required), loose-fitting clothing appropriate for the weather (goalkeepers wear a jersey in a different color), and shin guards worn under knee-length socks to protect players' legs. Gloves for goalkeepers have always been optional equipment, used predominately to grip the ball better rather than to protect the hands. In cold weather they can also help keep goalkeepers' hands warm and flexible for catching the ball.

Make sure that players on your team are outfitted properly and that the equipment they obtain meets acceptable standards. Advise players and their parents about how players' shoes should fit and how players should break shoes in when they are new. Occasionally inspect shin guards to be sure they are in good condition.

Player Positions

Give your young players a chance to play a variety of positions. By playing different positions, they'll have a better all-around playing experience and will stay more interested in the sport. Furthermore, they'll have a better understanding of the many technical and tactical skills used in the game. They will also better appreciate the efforts of their teammates who play positions they themselves find difficult.

Following are descriptions of the positions for soccer.

- *Forward:* Forwards play closer to the other team's goal and shoot the ball more than other players. The forwards that play nearest the touchlines are called wings; those in the middle of the field are referred to as strikers.
- *Midfielder:* Midfielders are all-purpose players who take shots and try to steal the ball from the other team. They are transition players, helping move the ball from defense to offense. Their position is named appropriately, since they play between forwards and defenders on the field.
- *Defender:* Defenders play near their own team's goal and try to prevent the other team from shooting the ball. They also receive the ball from the goalkeeper and move the ball up the field to begin the offense.

- *Goalkeeper*: A goalkeeper plays in front of the goal and tries to prevent the ball from getting into the goal. The goalkeeper is the only player allowed to use the hands to block shots and to initiate the offense from within the team's penalty area.

Soccer uses different alignments for different age groups (see table 3.1). In all cases, the numbers that describe team formation—as shown in the formation column of table 3.1—go from the back to the front, and the goalkeeper is assumed (except for the U6 and U8 age groups, for which no goalkeepers are used). For example, in the U14 age group, which uses 11 players on the field per team, a formation could be 4-3-3. These numbers mean 4 defenders, 3 midfielders, and 3 forwards. Please note, however, that these are not the only formations that can work with your players. You should choose a team formation that best executes the principles of play and that makes it easy for your players to support one another on offense and defense.

Table 3.1 Soccer Formations for Age Groups

Age group	Players on field	Formation used
U6	3v3	N/A
U8	4v4	Diamond or box
U10	6v6	3-2
U12	8v8	2-3-2
U14	11v11	3-4-3

For the U6 age group there is no team formation. Coaches of the U6 age group should not be dismayed if players tend to congregate around the ball simultaneously, because this is the nature of the age group. For the U8 age group, however, two formations—the diamond or the box—can be used. The diamond consists of 4 players assuming a diamondlike shape, with 1 player in back, 2 on the sides, and 1 in front. The box consists of 2 players in back and 2 players in front. In either case, remember that U8 players will have only slightly more understanding of group shape than the U6 age group, so don't be dismayed if they tend to stray from these formations and bunch around the ball.

The U10 through U14 age groups use more complex formations. For the U10 age group, you can use two basic formations—3 defenders and 2 forwards, or the reverse. For the U12 age group, three basic formations, a 3-2-2, a 3-3-1, or a 2-3-2, can be used. At this level, if the coach and team wish to forgo a midfield line, they can use a 4-3 formation. US Youth Soccer recommends the formation with 2 defenders, 3 midfielders, and 2 forwards. For the U14 age group, you can use two basic formations—a 4-3-3 or a 3-4-3. US Youth Soccer recommends the formation with 3 defenders, 4 midfielders, and 3 forwards.

Rules of Play

Soccer rules are designed to make the game run smoothly and safely and to prevent either team from gaining an unfair advantage. Following is an overview of some of the basic rules in soccer.

Starting the Game

Soccer games begin with one team, typically chosen by a coin toss, kicking the ball from the center mark. The opposing team's players are not allowed within the center circle during the kick-off. Players on both teams must be on their half of the field during the kickoff, and the kicked ball must roll forward at least one complete rotation before another player may touch it.

The same procedures are followed after a goal is scored. In this situation, the team that was scored on restarts the game by kicking off from the center mark, and the team that scored stands outside of the center circle in its half of the field.

Restarting the Game

Several situations may cause a referee to stop play during a game, and play must restart accordingly (depending on the reason for stopping play). Play is also stopped when a ball goes out of bounds beyond the goal line or along the touchline.

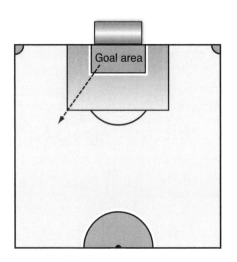

Figure 3.2   Goal kick location.

When an attacking team kicks the ball out of bounds beyond the goal line, as in a missed shot, the opposing team is awarded a free kick called a goal kick. The defending team makes this kick from anywhere inside the goal area. The majority of the time, the goal kick should be played upfield and out toward the touchlines, as shown in figure 3.2. The players on the team that kicked the ball out of bounds must stay outside the penalty area until the ball clears the area.

If a team kicks the ball beyond its own goal line, the other team is awarded a corner kick from the corner arc on the side of the field where the ball went out. During the kick, defensive players must be at least 10 yards, or a distance equivalent to the diameter of the center circle, from the player kicking the ball. The kicker's teammates may position themselves anywhere they choose. Corner kicks are most commonly made into three areas—the near post, the far post, and the penalty spot—as shown in figure 3.3.

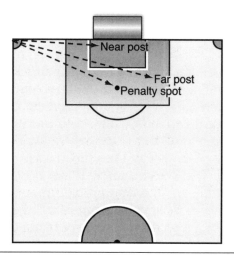

Figure 3.3 Corner kick locations.

When a player kicks the ball out of bounds along the touchline, the game is restarted with a throw-in at the spot where the ball went out (see figure 3.4). The team that last touched the ball loses possession, and the other team gets to throw in the ball. The player putting the ball back into play must use both hands to throw the ball and keep both feet on the ground. The throwing motion should begin from behind the head and maintain a continuous

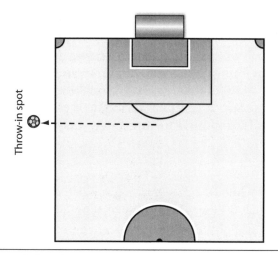

Figure 3.4 Throw-in location.

forward thrust until the ball is released in front of the head. The throw-in should be put into play quickly, thrown to the feet of a teammate who is not being marked.

Play is also stopped for no-penalty situations such as those mentioned in Soccer No-Nos on page 29. In these cases, play is restarted with a drop ball.

Goalkeeping

A goalkeeper, whose main responsibility is to stop shots on goal, is the last line of defense and the first line of offense. In youth soccer, as previously noted in this chapter, goalkeepers are not introduced until the U10 age group.

Goalkeepers may use their hands within their penalty area. They may also use their hands to collect a ball that a teammate has headed to them deliberately. Goalkeepers, however, may not use their hands to collect a ball that a teammate has kicked to them intentionally. When a goalkeeper catches a ball, she must release it within six to seven seconds. She may not touch the ball again before another player touches it outside of the penalty area. In addition, goalkeepers may not pick up a throw-in from a teammate.

Scoring

Each time the entire ball crosses the goal line between the goalposts and below the crossbar, the offensive team is awarded a goal. Scoring a goal is one of the tangible ways to measure personal performance. However, don't overemphasize goal scoring in assessing a player's contribution. Give equal attention to players who make assists, tackles, interceptions, or saves, and who demonstrate leadership, sporting behavior, and effort.

Rule Infractions

Although no soccer team will perform penalty free, teach your players to avoid recurring penalties. For example, if a penalty occurs in practice, stop the play and briefly discuss the result of the penalty. By instilling this discipline, you'll help players enjoy more success, both as individuals and as a team.

Following are several common infractions that soccer players commit:

Fouls

The referee calls a foul when one player charges, pushes, trips, kicks, or holds an opposing player. A handball foul is called when a player intentionally touches the ball with his hand or arm.

Players who keep fouling intentionally or playing dangerously are warned once by the referee. Persistent infractions may result in a yellow card caution.

The next time they intentionally foul or play dangerously, the referee gives them a red card and ejects them from the game. Officials can also eject a player without warning if they rule a behavior unacceptable.

Free Kicks

Fouls usually result in either a direct or an indirect free kick, depending on the type of foul (see table 3.2). Players may kick direct free kicks right to the goal, whereas indirect free kicks must touch a player other than the original kicker before a goal can be scored. Opponents must be at least 10 yards (or a distance equivalent to the diameter of the center circle) away from the ball during a free kick. Any free kick awarded within a defending team's own goal area may be taken from any point within the goal area. An indirect free kick awarded to the attacking team within the opponent's goal area will be taken from the line at the top of the goal area nearest to the point of infraction. The officials will signal which type of free kick has been awarded.

Table 3.2 Free Kick Fouls

Direct kick	Indirect kick
Handball	Playing dangerously
Kicking or attempting to kick an opponent	Obstruction
Striking	Goalkeeper taking more than 6 seconds to release the ball
Tripping an opponent	Offside
Holding an opponent	Goalkeeper touching the ball again with his hands after it has been released from his possession and has not yet been touched by a second player
Pushing an opponent	
Jumping at an opponent	Goalkeeper catching the ball on a throw-in from a teammate or after it has been kicked to her by a teammate
	Charging into or from behind an opponent

Penalty Kicks

Penalty kicks are awarded to the attacking team if a defending player commits a direct kick foul inside the penalty area. A penalty kick is a free shot at the goal by an individual attacker, with only the goalkeeper defending against the shot. Penalty kicks are taken from the penalty kick spot in front of the center of the goal, as shown in figure 3.1 on page 21. This distance is 10 yards for U12. For older participants, the distance is 12 yards. The goalkeeper may not leave the goal line until after the ball is kicked.

Offside

A player is in the offside position when he is closer to the opponent's goal than at least two defensive players, when the ball is passed forward. As you can see in figure 3.5, player 2 is offside. The offside rule prevents offensive players from simply waiting at the goalmouth for an easy shot, but it does not apply to throw-ins, corner kicks, or instances in which players are in their own half of the field. When a player is offside, the opposing team receives an indirect free kick at the point of the infraction.

Also, note that a player is not called offside merely for being in an offside position. The player must be participating in the play to be ruled offside. For example, if play is occurring on one side of the field, and a player on the other side of the field is in an offside position but is not involved in the play going on across the field (e.g., a teammate is not passing, or attempting to

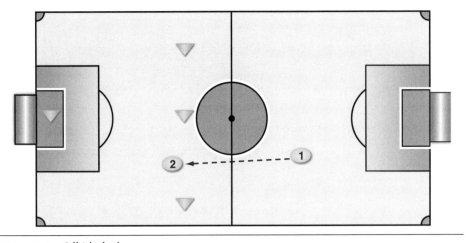

Figure 3.5 Offside foul.

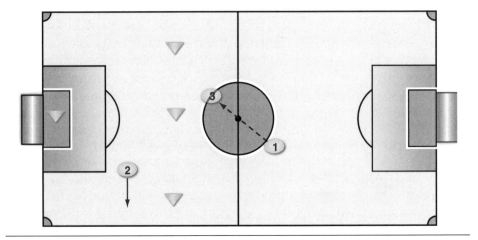

Figure 3.6 Offside—no call.

pass, to her), then that player won't be ruled offside. As you can see in figure 3.6, player 2 is not participating in the play and therefore is not in violation of the offside rule.

Soccer No-Nos

It is inevitable that your players will violate minor rules during practices and games now and then. But make clear to your players that some actions are considered bad sporting behavior and may result in a verbal warning or an ejection, depending on the severity or frequency of the infraction. These actions are the following:

- Removing the jersey during a goal celebration
- Feigning an injury or pretending to have been fouled
- Deliberately and blatantly handling the ball to prevent an opponent from gaining possession
- Holding an opponent to prevent him from gaining possession of the ball or taking up an advantageous position
- Delaying the game
- Excessive or time-wasting goal celebrating
- Making gestures that are provocative, derisory, or inflammatory
- Refusing to leave the field after the game has been stopped to deal with that player's injury

Officiating

Soccer officials enforce the rules. Their authority over a match begins at least 30 minutes before the start of play and finishes at least 30 minutes after it has ended. In youth soccer, there are typically three officials—a referee and two assistant referees—overseeing the game. For the U6 and U8 age groups there is often only one referee, and in many leagues even the coaches officiate. In the U10 age group, it is common for one certified referee to officiate the game because of the shortage of referees. It is also common for youngsters, some as young as 12 years old, to be the referees. Any official, however, has many responsibilities during a game, including effectively communicating the calls to other members of the referee crew and to the players, coaches, and spectators. See figure 3.7, *a* through *h*, for common officiating signals.

In addition, if you have a concern about how referees are officiating a game, address the officials respectfully. Do so immediately if at any time you feel that the officiating jeopardizes the safety of your players.

Figure 3.7 Officiating signals for *(a)* goal (points to center of field for kickoff), *(b)* penalty kick (points to penalty spot), *(c)* corner kick (points to corner arc), *(d)* goal kick (points to goal area), *(e)* advantage or play on, *(f)* offside or indirect free kick, *(g)* direct free kick, and *(h)* caution (yellow card) or ejection (red card).

Providing for Players' Safety

One of your players breaks free down the field, dribbling the ball. Suddenly a defender catches up with, and accidentally trips, the goalbound player. You notice that your player is not getting up from the ground and seems to be in pain. What do you do?

No coach wants to see players get hurt. But injury remains a reality of sport participation; consequently, you must be prepared to provide first aid when injuries occur and to protect yourself against unjustified lawsuits. Fortunately, coaches can institute many preventive measures to reduce the risks. In this chapter we describe steps you can take to prevent injuries, first aid and emergency responses you can carry out when injuries occur, and legal responsibilities you have as a coach.

Game Plan for Safety

You can't prevent all injuries from happening, but you can take preventive measures that give your players the best possible chance for injury-free participation. In creating the safest possible environment for your players, you can make preparations in these areas:

- Preseason physical examination
- Physical conditioning
- Equipment and facilities inspection
- Player matchups and inherent risks
- Proper supervision and record keeping
- Environmental conditions

Preseason Physical Examination

We recommend that your players have a physical examination before participating in soccer. The exam should address the most likely areas of medical concern and identify youngsters at high risk. We also suggest that you have players' parents or guardians sign a participation agreement form (this will be discussed in more detail later in this chapter) and an informed consent form to allow their children to be treated in case of an emergency. For a sample form, please see the Informed Consent Form on page 141.

Physical Conditioning

Players need to be in or get in shape to play the game at the level expected. They must have adequate cardiorespiratory and muscular fitness.

Cardiorespiratory fitness involves the body's ability to use oxygen and fuel efficiently to power muscle contractions. As players get in better shape, their bodies are able to deliver oxygen more efficiently to fuel muscles and carry off carbon dioxides and other wastes. Soccer requires lots of running and exertion; most players will move nearly continuously and make short bursts throughout a game. Youngsters who aren't as fit as their peers often overextend in trying to keep up, which can result in lightheadedness, nausea, fatigue, and potential injury.

Try to remember that the players' goals are to participate, learn, and have fun. Therefore you must keep your players active, attentive, and involved with every phase of practice. If you do, they will attain higher levels of cardiorespiratory fitness as the season progresses simply by taking part in practice. However, watch closely for signs of low cardiorespiratory fitness; don't let your players do much until they're fit. You might privately counsel youngsters who appear overly winded, suggesting that they train under proper supervision outside of practice to increase their fitness.

Muscular fitness encompasses strength, muscular endurance, power, speed, and flexibility. This type of fitness is affected by physical maturity, as well as by strength training and other types of training. Your players will likely exhibit a relatively wide range of muscular fitness. Those who have greater muscular fitness will be able to run faster and perform more consistently. They will also sustain fewer muscular injuries, and any injuries that do occur will tend to be minor. And in case of injury, recovery is faster in those with higher levels of muscular fitness.

> **Coaching Tip**
> Children aged 5 to 8 will play all out, with little or no sense of pace, and consequently will fatigue quickly. They will stop activity to rest, and when they resume they will go flat out again. Preadolescent children aged 5 to 15 will overheat sooner than an adult, so pay close attention to water breaks and to the climate in which practices and matches are taking place.

Two other components of fitness and injury prevention are the warm-up and the cool-down. Although young bodies are generally very limber, they can become tight through inactivity. The warm-up should address each muscle group and elevate the heart rate in preparation for strenuous activity. Players should warm up for 5 to 10 minutes using a combination of light running, jumping, and stretching. As practice winds down, slow players' heart rates with an easy jog or walk. Then have players stretch for 5 minutes to help prevent tight muscles before the next practice or match.

Equipment and Facilities Inspection

Another way to prevent injuries is to check the quality and fit of uniforms, practice attire, and protective equipment that your players use. Ensure that all players have adequate shin guards and that they wear them.

Remember also to regularly examine the field on which your players practice and play. Remove hazards, report conditions you cannot remedy, and request maintenance as necessary. If unsafe conditions exist, either make adaptations to prevent risk to your players' safety or stop the practice or game until safe conditions have been restored. Refer to appendix A for the Facilities and Equipment Checklist on page 140 to guide you in verifying that facilities are safe.

Player Matchups and Inherent Risks

We recommend that you group teams in two-year age increments if possible. You'll encounter fewer mismatches in physical maturation with narrow age ranges. Even so, two 12-year-old boys might differ by 90 pounds in weight, a foot in height, and three or four years in emotional and intellectual maturity. Such variation presents dangers for the less mature. Closely supervise games so that the more mature do not put the less mature at undue risk.

Although proper matching of age groups helps protect you from certain liability concerns, you must also warn players of the inherent risks involved in playing soccer, because failure to warn is one of the most successful arguments in lawsuits against coaches. Please note that although soccer is not a collision sport, it is a contact sport and injuries are possible. Thoroughly explain the inherent risks of soccer and make sure each player knows, understands, and appreciates the risks. You can learn more about intrinsic risks by talking with your league administrators.

The preseason orientation meeting for parents is a good opportunity to explain the risks of the sport to both parents and players. It is also a good occasion on which to have both the players and their parents sign a participation agreement form or waiver releasing you from liability should an injury occur. You should work with your league when creating these forms or waivers, and legal counsel should review them prior to presentation. These documents do not relieve you of responsibility for your players' well-being, but lawyers recommend them and they may help you in the event of a lawsuit.

Coaching Tip

Coed teams are perfectly acceptable up until puberty (generally the U12 age group). In the U6 and U8 age groups there are few differences between females and males in height and weight.

Proper Supervision and Record Keeping

To ensure players' safety, you must provide both general supervision and specific supervision. General supervision means that you are in the area of activity so that you can see and hear what is happening. You should be

- on the field and in position to supervise the players even before the formal practice begins,
- immediately accessible to the activity and able to oversee the entire activity,
- alert to conditions that may be dangerous to players and ready to take action to protect players,

- able to react immediately and appropriately to emergencies, and
- present on the field until the last player has been picked up after the practice or game.

Specific supervision is the direct supervision of an activity at practice. For example, you should provide specific supervision when you teach new skills and continue it until your players understand the requirements of the activity, the risks involved, and their own ability to perform in light of these risks. You must also provide specific supervision when you notice players breaking rules or see a change in the condition of your players. As a general rule, the more dangerous the activity, the more specific the supervision required. This principle suggests that younger and less experienced players require more specific supervision.

> **Coaching Tip**
> Although six-year-olds do indeed need a good bit of supervision during practices and games, they do not generate the force or velocity that teenage players do in respect to impact injuries. They bump into one another, which may cause tears to appear, but it is less likely that a serious injury has occurred. You must attentively supervise all activity, of all age groups, at all training sessions and matches.

As part of your supervisory duties, you are expected to foresee potentially dangerous situations and to help prevent them. This responsibility requires that you know soccer well, especially the rules that are intended to provide for safety. For example, serious injury and possibly death can occur if a goal topples over onto a player. So prohibit dangerous horseplay and hold training sessions only under safe weather conditions. Such specific supervisory activities, applied consistently, will make the play environment safer for your players and will help protect you from liability if a mishap occurs.

For further protection, keep records of your season plans, practice plans, and players' injuries. Season and practice plans come in handy when you need evidence that you have taught players certain skills, and accurate, detailed injury report forms offer protection against unfounded lawsuits. Ask for these forms from your sponsoring organization (see page 142 in appendix A for a sample injury report form), and hold onto these records for several years so that a past soccer injury of a former player doesn't come back to haunt you.

Environmental Conditions

Most health problems that environmental factors cause are related to excessive heat or cold, but you should also consider other environmental factors such as severe weather and air pollution. A little thought about the potential problems and a little effort to ensure adequate protection for your players will prevent most serious emergencies related to environmental conditions.

Heat

On hot, humid days the body has difficulty cooling itself. Because the air is already saturated with water vapor (humidity), sweat doesn't evaporate as easily. Therefore body sweat is a less effective cooling agent, and the body retains extra heat. Hot, humid environments put players at risk of heat exhaustion and heatstroke (see more on these in Serious Injuries on pages 43-44). And if *you* think it's hot or humid, it's worse for the kids, not only because they're more active but also because kids under the age of 12 have more difficulty regulating their body temperature than do adults. To provide for players' safety in hot or humid conditions, take the following preventive measures.

Coaching Tip

Encourage players to drink plenty of water before, during, and after practice. Water makes up 45 to 65 percent of a youngster's body weight, and losing even a small amount of water can cause severe consequences in the body's systems. It doesn't have to be hot and humid for players to become dehydrated, nor is thirst an accurate indicator. In fact, by the time players are aware of their thirst they are long overdue for a drink.

- Monitor weather conditions and adjust training sessions accordingly. Table 4.1 shows the specific air temperatures and humidity percentages that can be hazardous to players.

- Acclimatize players to exercising in high heat and humidity. Players can adjust to high heat and humidity in 7 to 10 days. During this period, hold practices at low to moderate levels of activity and give the players fluid breaks every 20 minutes.

- Switch to light clothing. Players should wear shorts and white T-shirts.

- Identify and monitor players who are prone to heat illness. Players who are overweight, heavily muscled, or out of shape and players who work excessively hard or have experienced previous heat illness are more prone to getting heat illness. Closely monitor these children and give them fluid breaks every 15 to 20 minutes, or even more frequently for the U6 age group.

Table 4.1   Warm-Weather Precautions

Temperature (°F)	Humidity	Precautions
80-90	<70%	Monitoring of athletes prone to heat illness
	>70%	5 min rest after 30 min of practice
90-100	<70%	5 min rest after 30 min of practice
	>70%	Short practices in evening or early morning

- Make sure players replace fluids lost through sweat. Encourage players to drink 17 to 20 ounces of fluid 2 to 3 hours before practices or games and 7 to 10 ounces every 20 minutes during and after practice. Afterward they should drink 16 to 24 ounces of fluid for every pound lost during exercise. Fluids such as water and sports drinks are preferable during games and practices (suggested intakes are based on National Athletic Trainers' Association [NATA] recommendations). The amount of fluid is generally the same for each age group; however, prepubescent players should drink more water than sports drinks.

- Replenish electrolytes, such as sodium (salt) and potassium, which are lost through sweat. The best way to replace these nutrients in addition to others such as carbohydrate (for energy) and protein (for muscle building) is by eating a balanced diet. Experts say that during the most intense training periods in the heat, additional salt intake may be helpful in replenishing electrolytes.

Cold

When a person is exposed to cold weather, body temperature starts to drop below normal. To counteract this reaction, the body shivers to create heat and reduces blood flow to the extremities to conserve heat in the core of the body. But no matter how effective its natural heating mechanism is, the body will better withstand cold temperatures if it is prepared to handle them. To reduce the risk of cold-related illnesses, make sure players wear appropriate protective clothing and keep them active to maintain body heat. Also monitor the windchill factor, because it can drastically affect the severity of players' responses to the weather. The windchill factor index is shown in table 4.2.

Table 4.2   Windchill Factor Index

Temperature (°F)

Wind speed (mph)	0	5	10	15	20	25	30	35	40
	Flesh may freeze within one minute								
40	-55	-45	-35	-30	-20	-15	-5	0	10
35	-50	-40	-35	-30	-20	-10	-5	5	10
30	-50	-40	-30	-25	-20	-10	0	5	10
25	-45	-35	-30	-20	-15	-5	0	10	15
20	-35	-30	-25	-15	-10	0	5	10	20
15	-30	-25	-20	-10	-5	0	10	15	25
10	-20	-15	-10	0	5	10	15	20	30
5	-5	0	5	10	15	20	25	30	35

Windchill temperature (°F)

Severe Weather

Severe weather refers to a host of potential dangers, including lightning storms, tornadoes, hail, and heavy rains. Lightning is of special concern because it can come up quickly and cause great harm, or even kill. For each 5-second count from the flash of lightning to the bang of thunder, lightning is one mile away. A flash-bang of 10 seconds means lightning is two miles away; a flash-bang of 15 seconds indicates lightning is three miles away. You should stop a practice or competition for the day if lightning is three miles away or closer (15 seconds or less from flash to bang). Your school or club, league, or state association may have additional rules that you will want to consider in severe weather.

Safe places in which to take cover when lightning strikes are fully enclosed metal vehicles with the windows up, enclosed buildings, and low ground (under cover of bushes, if possible). It's not safe to be near metal objects such as flag poles, fences, light poles, goals, and metal bleachers. Also avoid trees, water, and open fields.

Cancel practice when under a tornado watch or warning. If you are practicing or competing when a tornado is nearby, you should get inside a building if possible. If you cannot get into a building, lie down in a ditch or other low-lying area or crouch near a strong building and use your arms to protect your head and neck.

The keys to handling severe weather are caution and prudence. Don't try to get that last 10 minutes of practice in if lightning is on the horizon. Don't continue to play in heavy rain. Many storms can strike both quickly and ferociously. Respect the weather and play it safe.

Air Pollution

Poor air quality and smog can present real dangers to your players. Both short- and long-term lung damage are possible from exercising in unsafe air. Although it's true that exercising in clean air is not possible in many areas, restricting activity is recommended when the air quality ratings are lower than moderate or when there is a smog alert. Your local health department or air quality control board can inform you of the air quality ratings for your area and of their recommendations for when to restrict activities.

Responding to Players' Injuries

No matter how good and thorough your prevention program is, injuries quite likely will occur. When injury does strike, chances are you will be the one in charge. The severity and nature of the injury will determine how actively involved you'll be in treating it. But regardless of how seriously a player is hurt, it is your responsibility to know what steps to take. Therefore, you must be prepared to take appropriate action and provide basic emergency care when an injury occurs.

Being Prepared

Being prepared to provide basic emergency care involves many elements, including being trained in cardiopulmonary resuscitation (CPR) and first aid and having an emergency plan.

First-Aid Kit

A well-stocked first-aid kit should include the following:

- Antibacterial soap or wipes
- Arm sling
- Athletic tape—one and a half inches wide
- Bandage scissors
- Bandage strips—assorted sizes
- Blood spill kit
- Cell phone
- Contact lens case
- Cotton swabs
- Elastic wraps—three inches, four inches, and six inches
- Emergency blanket
- Examination gloves—latex-free
- Eye patch
- Foam rubber—one-eighth inch, one-fourth inch, and one-half inch
- Insect sting kit
- List of emergency phone numbers
- Mirror
- Moleskin
- Nail clippers
- Oral thermometer (to determine whether a player has a fever caused by illness)
- Penlight
- Petroleum jelly
- Plastic bags for crushed ice
- Prewrap (underwrap for tape)
- Rescue breathing or CPR face mask
- Safety glasses (for first aiders)
- Safety pins
- Saline solution for eyes
- Sterile gauze pads—three-inch and four-inch squares (preferably nonstick)
- Sterile gauze rolls
- Sunscreen—sun protection factor (SPF) 30 or greater
- Tape adherent and tape remover
- Tongue depressors
- Tooth saver kit
- Triangular bandages
- Tweezers

Adapted, by permission, from M. Flegel, 2004, *Sport first aid,* 3rd ed. (Champaign, IL: Human Kinetics), 20.

CPR and First-Aid Training

We recommend that all coaches receive CPR and first-aid training from a nationally recognized organization such as the National Safety Council, the American Heart Association, the American Red Cross, or the American Sport Education Program (ASEP). You should be certified based on both a practical test and a written test of knowledge. Training in CPR should include obstructed airway procedures and basic life support for both children and adults.

Emergency Plan

An emergency plan is the final tool for being prepared to take appropriate action for severe or serious injuries. The plan calls for three steps:

1. *Evaluate the injured player.*

   Use your CPR and first-aid training to guide you. Be sure to keep these certifications up to date. Practice your skills frequently to keep them fresh and ready to use when you need them.

2. *Call the appropriate medical personnel.*

   If possible, delegate the responsibility of seeking medical help to another calm and responsible adult who attends all practices and games. Write out a list of emergency phone numbers and keep it with you at practices and games. Include the following phone numbers:

   - Rescue unit
   - Hospital
   - Physician
   - Police
   - Fire department

   Take each player's emergency information to every practice and game (see Emergency Information Card in appendix A on page 143). This information includes the person to contact in case of an emergency, what types of medications the player is using, what types of drugs the player is allergic to, and so on.

   Give an emergency response card (see Emergency Response Card in appendix A on page 144) to the contact person calling for emergency assistance. Having this information ready should help the contact person remain calm. You must also complete an injury report form (see appendix A) and keep it on file for any injury that occurs.

3. *Provide first aid.*

   If medical personnel are not on hand at the time of the injury, provide first-aid care to the extent of your qualifications. Although your CPR and first-aid training will guide you, you must remember the following:

   - Do not move the injured player if the injury is to the head, neck, or back; if a large joint (ankle, knee, elbow, shoulder) is dislocated; or if the pelvis, a rib, an arm, or a leg is fractured.
   - Calm the injured player and keep others away from him as much as possible.
   - Evaluate whether the player's breathing has stopped or is irregular and clear the airway with your fingers if necessary.

- Administer artificial respiration if the player's breathing has stopped. Administer CPR if the player's circulation has stopped.
- Remain with the player until medical personnel arrive.

Emergency Steps

You need to have a clear, well-rehearsed emergency action plan. You want to be sure you are prepared in case of an emergency, because every second counts. Your emergency plan should follow this sequence:

1. Check the player's level of consciousness.
2. Send a contact person to call the appropriate medical personnel and the player's parents.
3. Send someone to wait for the rescue team and direct them to the injured player.
4. Assess the injury.
5. Administer first aid.
6. Assist emergency medical personnel in preparing the player for transportation to a medical facility.
7. Appoint someone to go with the player if the parents are not available. This person should be responsible, calm, and familiar with the player. Assistant coaches or parents are best for this job.
8. Complete an injury report form while the incident is fresh in your mind (see page 142 in appendix A).

Taking Appropriate Action

Proper CPR and first-aid training, a well-stocked first-aid kit, and an emergency plan prepare you to take appropriate action when an injury occurs. We spoke in the previous section about the importance of providing first aid to the extent of your qualifications. Don't play doctor with injuries; sort out minor injuries that you can treat from those that need medical attention. Let's take a look at the appropriate actions for minor injuries and more serious injuries.

Minor Injuries

Although no injury seems minor to the person experiencing it, most injuries are neither life threatening nor severe enough to restrict participation. When these injuries occur, you can take an active role in their initial treatment.

Scrapes and Cuts   When one of your players has an open wound, the first thing you should do is put on a pair of disposable latex-free examination gloves or some other effective blood barrier. Then follow these four steps:

Coaching Tip

You shouldn't let a fear of exposing yourself to HIV (human immunodeficiency virus), the cause of AIDS (acquired immunodeficiency syndrome), or contracting other communicable diseases stop you from helping a player. You are only at risk if you allow contaminated blood to come in contact with an open wound on your body; the examination gloves that you wear will protect you should one of your players carry HIV or other infectious illnesses. Check with your sport director, your league, or the Centers for Disease Control and Prevention (CDC) for more information about protecting yourself and your participants from HIV exposure.

1. Stop the bleeding by applying direct pressure to the wound with a clean dressing and elevating it. The player may be able to apply this pressure while you put on your gloves. Do not remove the dressing if it becomes soaked with blood. Instead, place an additional dressing on top of the one already in place. If bleeding continues, elevate the injured area above the heart and maintain pressure.

2. Cleanse the wound thoroughly once the bleeding is controlled. A good rinsing with a forceful stream of water, and perhaps light scrubbing with soap, will help prevent infection.

3. Protect the wound with sterile gauze or a bandage strip. If the player continues to participate, apply protective padding over the injured area.

4. Remove and dispose of gloves carefully to prevent you or anyone else from coming into contact with blood.

For bloody noses not associated with serious facial injury, have the player sit and lean slightly forward. Then pinch the player's nostrils shut. If the bleeding continues after several minutes, or if the player has a history of nosebleeds, seek medical assistance.

Strains and Sprains   The physical demands of soccer training and games often result in injuries to the muscles or tendons (strains) or to the ligaments (sprains). When your players suffer minor strains or sprains, immediately apply the PRICE method of injury care:

P   Protect the player and the injured body part from further danger or trauma.

R   Rest the area to avoid further damage and foster healing.

I   Ice the area to reduce swelling and pain.

C   Compress the area by securing an ice bag in place with an elastic wrap.

E   Elevate the injury above heart level to keep blood from pooling in the area.

Bumps and Bruises   Soccer players inevitably make contact with each other and with the ground. If the force applied to a body part at impact is great enough, a bump or bruise will result. Many players continue playing with such sore spots, but if the bump or bruise is large and painful, you should act appropriately. Again, use the PRICE method for injury care and monitor the injury. If swelling, discoloration, and pain have lessened, the player may resume participation with protective padding; if not, the player should be examined by a physician.

Serious Injuries

Head, neck, and back injuries; fractures; and injuries that cause a player to lose consciousness are among a class of injuries that you cannot and should not try to treat yourself. In these cases you should follow the emergency plan outlined on page 40. We do want to examine more closely, however, your role in preventing heat cramps, heat exhaustion, and heatstroke. Additionally, please refer to figure 4.1 for an illustrative example of the signs and symptoms associated with heat exhaustion and heatstroke.

Heat Cramps   Tough practices combined with heat stress and substantial fluid loss from sweating can provoke muscle cramps commonly known as heat cramps. Cramping is most common during the early part of the season, when weather is the hottest and players may be least adapted to heat. The cramp, a severe tightening of the muscle, can drop players and prevent continued play. Dehydration, electrolyte loss, and fatigue are the contributing factors. The immediate treatment is to have players cool off and slowly stretch the contracted muscle. Players may return to play later that same day or the next day, provided the cramp doesn't cause a muscle strain.

Heat Exhaustion   Heat exhaustion is a shocklike condition caused by dehydration and electrolyte depletion. Symptoms include headache, nausea, dizziness, chills, fatigue, and extreme thirst. Profuse sweating is a key sign of heat exhaustion. Other signs include pale, cool, clammy skin; rapid, weak pulse; loss of coordination; and dilated pupils.

A player with heat exhaustion should rest in a cool, shaded area; drink cool fluids, particularly those containing electrolytes; and apply ice to the neck, back, or abdomen to help cool the body. If you believe a player has heat exhaustion, seek medical attention. Under no conditions should the player return to activity that day or before she regains all the weight lost through sweating. If the player has to see a physician, she shouldn't return to the team until she has a written release from the physician.

Heatstroke   Heatstroke is a life-threatening condition in which the body stops sweating and body temperature rises dangerously high. It occurs when dehydration causes a malfunction in the body's temperature control center in the brain. Symptoms include the feeling of being extremely hot, nausea, confusion, irritability, and fatigue. Signs include hot, dry, and flushed or red skin (this is a key sign), lack of sweat, rapid pulse, rapid breathing, constricted pupils, vomiting, diarrhea, and possibly seizures, unconsciousness, or respiratory or cardiac arrest.

If you suspect a player has heatstroke, send for emergency medical assistance immediately and cool the player as quickly as possible. Remove excess clothing and equipment from the player and cool his body by using cool, wet towels, by pouring cool water over him, or by placing him in a cold water bath. Apply ice packs to the armpits, neck, back, and abdomen and between the legs. If the player is conscious, give him cool fluids to drink. If the player is unconscious, place him on his side to allow fluids and vomit to drain from the mouth. A player who has suffered heatstroke may not return to the team until he has a written release from a physician.

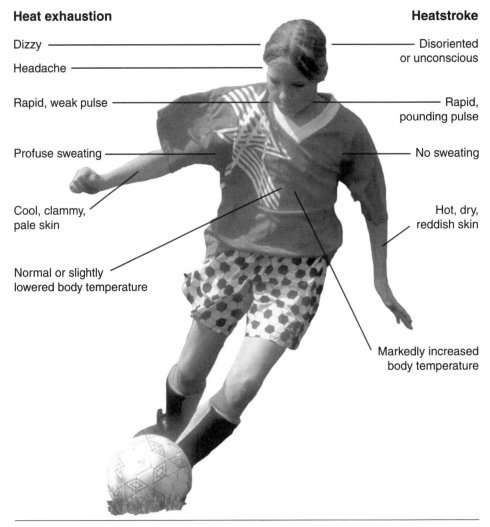

Heat exhaustion

Dizzy

Headache

Rapid, weak pulse

Profuse sweating

Cool, clammy,
pale skin

Normal or slightly
lowered body temperature

Heatstroke

Disoriented
or unconscious

Rapid,
pounding pulse

No sweating

Hot, dry,
reddish skin

Markedly increased
body temperature

Figure 4.1   Signs and symptoms of heat exhaustion and heatstroke.

Protecting Yourself

When one of your players is injured, naturally your first concern is that player's well-being. Your feelings for youngsters, after all, are what made you decide to coach. Unfortunately, you must consider something else: Can you be held liable for the injury?

From a legal standpoint, a coach must fulfill nine duties. We've discussed all but planning in this chapter (planning will be discussed in chapters 5 and 10). The following is a summary of your legal duties:

1. Provide a safe environment.
2. Properly plan the activity.
3. Provide adequate and proper equipment.
4. Match players.
5. Warn of inherent risks in the sport.
6. Supervise the activity closely.
7. Evaluate players for injury or incapacitation.
8. Know emergency procedures, CPR, and first aid.
9. Keep adequate records.

In addition to fulfilling these nine legal duties, you should check your organization's insurance coverage and your own insurance coverage to make sure these policies will properly protect you from liability.

5

Making Practices Fun and Practical

n the past we have placed too much emphasis on learning skills and not enough on learning how to play skillfully—that is, learning how to use those skills in competition. The games approach, in contrast to the traditional approach, emphasizes first learning what to do, then how to do it. Moreover, the games approach lets kids discover what to do in the game not by your telling them but by their experiencing it. It is a guided discovery method of teaching that empowers your players to solve the problems that arise in the game, which is a large part of the fun in learning. The games approach, in time, helps to develop a soccer-savvy player. Being soccer savvy means that a player has an innate understanding of what is going on around her on a soccer field and has the talent to influence the game. Such an outcome can only occur if the soccer environment in which the player is trained is a rich one. The use of guided discovery by coaches will be a positive influence on this healthy soccer experience.

On the surface, it seems to make sense to introduce soccer using the traditional approach—by first teaching the basic skills of the sport and then the tactics of the game. This approach, however, has disadvantages. First, it teaches the skills of the sport out of the context of the game. Kids may learn to control, shoot, pass, dribble, and head the ball. But they find it difficult to use these skills in the real game, because they do not yet understand the fundamental tactics of soccer and do not appreciate how best to use their newfound skills. Second, learning skills by doing drills outside of the context of the game is downright boring. The single biggest turnoff in sports is overly organized instruction that deprives kids of their intrinsic desire to play the game. See table 5.1 for a comparison of the use of drills versus activities in soccer.

Table 5.1   Drills Versus Activities

Drills	Activities
Static	Dynamic
Military	Unstructured
Lines	Free movement
Boring	Fun
No thought	Decision making
Age inappropriate	Age appropriate

The games approach is taught using a four-step process:

1. Play a modified game.
2. Help the players discover what they need to do in order to play the game successfully.

3. Teach the skills of the game.

4. Practice the skills in another game.

Step 1: Play a Modified Game

It's the first day of training; some of the kids are eager to get started, whereas others are obviously apprehensive. Some have rarely kicked a ball, most don't know the rules, and none know the positions in soccer. What do you do?

First, base all practices on the season and practice plans that you will learn more about in chapter 10. For example, if you used the traditional approach you would have players practice kicking by lining them up for a simple kicking drill. With the games approach, however, you begin by playing an even-sided game, such as 4v4, that is modified to be developmentally appropriate for the level of the players and is designed to focus on learning a specific part of the game (such as kicking).

Modifying the game emphasizes a limited number of game situations. This is one way you guide your players to discover certain tactics in the game. For instance, you have your players play a 2v2 game in a 20-by-15-yard playing area. The objective of the game is to make four passes before attempting to score. Playing the game this way forces players to think about what they have to do to keep possession of the ball.

Activities Checklist

When developing activities for your youth soccer program, here are a few questions that you should ask yourself.

- Are the activities fun?
- Are the activities organized?
- Are the players involved in the activities?
- Are creativity and decision making being used?
- Are the spaces used appropriate?
- Is the coach's feedback appropriate?
- Are there implications for the game?

Step 2: Help Players Understand the Game

As your players are playing a game, look for the right spot to freeze the action, step in, and ask questions about errors that you're seeing. When you do so, you help them better understand the objective of the game, what they must do to reach the objective, and what specific skills they must use.

Asking the right questions is an important part of teaching. You'll be asking your players (usually literally), "What do you need to do to succeed in this situation?" Sometimes players simply need to have more time playing to discover what they are to do, or you may need to further modify the game to make it even easier for them. This approach may take more patience on your part, but it's a powerful way for kids to learn. For example, assume your players are playing a game in which the objective is to make four passes before attempting to score, but they are having trouble doing so. Interrupt the action and ask the following questions:

- What are you supposed to do in this game?
- What does your team have to do to keep the ball for four passes in a row?
- What do you need to do when you pass the ball to help your team keep the ball?
- Where would you move to when your teammate has the ball and you need to help him keep the ball?

Coaching Tip

The atmosphere that a coach creates is crucial to learning. Players must see the soccer environment as physically and psychologically safe. The atmosphere should be comfortable for everyone and should not cater exclusively to the elite players. Approachability and a nonjudgmental attitude encourage players to take risks, one of which is to continue with soccer.

If your players have trouble understanding what to do, phrase your questions to let them choose between one option and another. For example, if you ask, "What's the fastest way to get the ball down the field?" and get answers such as "Throw it" or "Kick it," then ask, "Is it passing or dribbling?"

Asking the right questions may seem difficult at first, because your players have little or no experience with the game. If you've learned sport through the traditional approach, you'll be tempted to tell your players how to play the game rather than wasting time asking questions. Resist this powerful temptation to tell your players what to do. Instead, through the modified games approach and skillful questioning on your part, your players should come to realize on their own that accurate passing and receiving skills are essential to their success in controlling the ball. Rather than having told them what the critical skills are, you will have led them to this discovery—a crucial process in the games approach. Although it takes longer to teach a ball skill or tactic to players in the discovery games approach to practice, what they learn sticks more permanently and develops more self-reliant players.

Step 3: Teach the Skills of the Game

Only when your players recognize the skills they need to be successful in the game do you teach specific skills through activities that focus solely on the skill at hand. This is the time when you temporarily use a more traditional approach to teaching sport skills—the IDEA approach, which we will describe in chapter 6.

Step 4: Practice the Skills in Another Game

As a coach, you want your players to experience success as they're learning skills, and the best way to help them experience success early on is to create an advantage for the players. Once the players have practiced the skill as outlined in step 3, you can then put them in another game situation—this time an uneven numbers game (e.g., 3v1, 3v2). The prevailing notion is that this concept makes it more likely that, for instance, in a 3v1 game, your three offensive players will be able to make four passes before attempting to score.

We recommend first using even-sided games (e.g., 3v3, 6v6), as discussed in step 1, and then uneven-sided games. The purpose behind this method is to introduce players to a situation similar to what they will experience in competition and let them discover the challenges they face in performing the necessary skill. Then you teach them the skill, have them practice it, and put them back in another game—this time using an uneven advantage to give them a greater chance of experiencing success.

As players improve their skills, however, you may not need to use uneven-sided games. A 3v1 or 6v3 advantage will eventually become too easy and won't challenge your players to hone their skills. When this time comes, you can lessen the advantage. You may even decide that they're ready to practice the skill in even-sided competition. The key is to set up situations in which your athletes experience success but are challenged at the same time. This method will take careful monitoring on your part, but having kids play uneven games as they are learning skills is a very effective way of helping them learn and improve.

The ultimate goal, of course, is to develop more soccer-savvy players who are more self-reliant during a match. Players consistently coached with the games approach will be more adaptable to the demands of the game, and this coaching method is also more likely to produce creative players. When the atmosphere at a training session is permeated with positive interaction, creativity, and well-timed questions, players will arrive at training already mentally alert.

That's the games approach. It immerses players in the fun of playing soccer, thus motivating them to learn the skills that will help them play the game better. Consider the difference between reciting verb conjugations in a language class but not being allowed to try to communicate in the language versus trying out some brief social communications in the language (e.g., where's the bathroom, how do I get to the restaurant) and thereby understanding that getting the form of the verbs right matters. Learning skills in the context of playing modified games lets players discover the whys and the hows of soccer in the same fun environment. Your players will get to play more in practice, and once they learn how the skills fit into their performance and enjoyment of the game, they'll be enthusiastic about working on the skills you teach them.

6

Teaching and Shaping Skills

Coaching soccer is about teaching kids how to play the game by teaching them skills, fitness, fair play, and values. It's also about coaching players before, during, and after matches. Teaching and coaching are closely related, but there are important differences. In this chapter we focus on principles of teaching, especially teaching technical and tactical skills. But these principles apply to teaching fitness concepts and values as well. Armed with these principles, you will be able to design effective and efficient practices and will understand how to deal with misbehavior. Then you will be able to teach the skills and plays necessary to be successful in soccer, which are outlined in chapters 7 and 8.

Teaching Soccer Skills

Many people believe that the only qualification needed to teach a skill is to have performed it. Although it's helpful to have performed the skill, teaching it successfully requires much more than that. Even if you haven't performed the skill before, you can still learn to teach successfully with the useful acronym IDEA:

I   Introduce the skill.

D   Demonstrate the skill.

E   Explain the skill.

A   Attend to players practicing the skill.

Introduce the Skill

Players, especially those who are young and inexperienced, need to know what skill they are learning and why they are learning it. You should therefore use the following three steps every time you introduce a skill to your players:

1. Get your players' attention.
2. Name the skill.
3. Explain the importance of the skill.

Get Your Players' Attention

Because youngsters are easily distracted, you must make them sit up and take notice. Some coaches use interesting news items or stories, others use jokes, and still others simply project enthusiasm to get their players to listen. Whatever method you use, speak slightly above your normal volume and look your players in the eye when you speak.

Also, position players so that they can see and hear you. Arrange them in two or three evenly spaced rows, facing you (make sure they aren't looking into the sun or at a distracting activity). Then ask whether all of them can see you before you begin to speak.

> **Coaching Tip**
> Writing out in detail each skill you will teach clarifies what you will say and how you will demonstrate each skill to your players.

Name the Skill

Although there may be other common names for the skill you are introducing, decide as a staff before the start of the season which one you'll use and stick with it. Doing so prevents confusion and enhances communication among your players. When you introduce the new skill, call it by name several times so that the players automatically correlate the name with the skill in later discussions.

Explain the Importance of the Skill

As Rainer Martens, the founder of ASEP, has said, "The most difficult aspect of coaching is this: Coaches must learn to let athletes learn. Sport skills should be taught so they have meaning to the child, not just meaning to the coach." Although the importance of a skill may be apparent to you, your players may be less able to see how the skill will help them become better soccer players. Offer them a reason for learning the skill and describe how it relates to more advanced skills. This step will increase in importance from the U10 age group on up. For the U6 and U8 age groups, you may want to use imagination and storytelling to introduce skills into gamelike activities.

Demonstrate the Skill

The demonstration step is the most important part of teaching sport skills to players who may never have done anything closely resembling it. They need to see how the skill is performed, not just to hear a description. If you are unable to perform the skill correctly, ask an assistant coach, one of your players, or someone more skilled to demonstrate it.

These tips will make your demonstrations more effective:

- Use correct form.
- Demonstrate the skill several times.
- Slow the action, if possible, during one or two performances so that players can see every movement involved in the skill.
- Perform the skill at different angles so that your players can get a range of perspectives.
- Demonstrate the skill with both sides of the body, as applicable.
- Do not speak during the demonstration; save your words for before and after you demonstrate.

Explain the Skill

Players learn more effectively when they're given a brief explanation of the skill along with the demonstration. Use simple terms and, if possible, relate the skill to those previously learned. Ask your players whether they understand your description. A good technique is to ask the team to repeat your explanation. Ask questions like "What are you going to do first?" and "Then what?" Should players look confused or uncertain, repeat your explanation and demonstration. If possible, use different words so that your players can try to understand the skill from a different perspective. Remember, too, that whenever you bring players into a group to make a coaching point, you must be clear and concise.

Coaching Tip
Demonstrations should take 1 minute or less in order to keep the attention of the players. For the U8 and U10 age groups, try to keep demonstrations at 30 seconds or less, and for the U6 age group, try to keep demonstrations at 15 seconds or less.

Complex skills often are better understood when you explain them in more manageable parts. For instance, if you want to teach your players how to change direction when they dribble the ball, you might take the following steps:

1. Show players a correct performance of the entire skill and explain its function in soccer.
2. Break down the skill and point out its component parts to your players.
3. Have players perform each of the component skills you have already taught them, such as dribbling while running, changing speed, and changing direction.
4. After players have demonstrated their ability to perform the separate parts of the skill in sequence, explain the entire skill again.
5. Have players practice the skill in gamelike conditions.

Young players have short attention spans, and a long demonstration or explanation of a skill may cause them to lose focus. Therefore, spend no more than a few minutes altogether on the introduction, demonstration, and explanation phases. Then involve the players in activities that call on them to perform the skill.

Attend to Players Practicing the Skill

If the skill you selected was within your players' capabilities and you have done an effective job of introducing, demonstrating, and explaining it, your players should be ready to attempt the skill. Some players may need to be physically guided through the movements during their first few attempts.

How to Properly Run Your Activities

Before running an activity that teaches technique, you should do the following:

- Name the activity.
- Explain the skill you are teaching.
- Position the players correctly.
- Explain what the activity will accomplish. This step is important for the U12 and older age groups.
- State the command that will start the activity.
- State the command that will end the activity.

Once you have introduced and repeated the activity a few times in this manner, you will find that merely calling out the name of the activity is sufficient. Your players will automatically line up in the proper position to run the activity and practice the skill.

Walking unsure athletes through the skill in this way will help them gain confidence to perform it on their own. Please be aware that trial and error is an important part of learning any physical skill. Be patient as players make mistakes learning a skill; many soccer skills can take years to fully master.

Look at the entire skill and then break it down into fundamental components. For example, when teaching the push pass, your activity sequence could consist of the following steps:

1. Stance
2. Back swing of the kicking leg
3. Forward swing of the kicking leg
4. Proper contact with the ball
5. Follow-through of the kicking leg
6. Pattern recognition and pattern reaction

Your teaching duties, though, don't end when all your players have demonstrated that they understand how to perform a skill. As you help your players improve their skills, your teaching role is in fact just beginning. A significant part of coaching consists of closely observing the hit-and-miss trial performances of your players. You will sharpen players' skills by detecting errors and correcting them with positive feedback. Keep in mind that your positive feedback will have a great influence on your players' motivation to practice and improve their performances. Focus your attention and comments on catching them being good rather than on the inevitable miscues.

Remember, too, that some players may need individual instruction. So set aside a time before, during, or after practice to give individual help.

Helping Players Improve Skills

After you have successfully taught your players the fundamentals of a skill, your focus will be on helping them improve it. Players learn skills and improve them at different rates, so don't get frustrated if progress seems slow. Instead, help them progress by shaping their skills and detecting and correcting errors.

Shaping Players' Skills

One of your principal teaching duties is to reward positive effort and behavior—in terms of successful skill execution—when you see it. A player makes a good pass in practice, and you immediately say, "That's the way to drive through it! Good follow-through!" Such comments, plus a smile and a thumbs-up gesture, go a long way toward reinforcing skill technique in that player. However, sometimes you may have a long dry spell before you see correct techniques to reinforce. It's difficult to reward players when they don't execute skills correctly. How can you shape their skills if this is the case?

Molding skills takes practice on your players' part and patience on yours. Expect them to make errors. Telling the player who made the great pass that he did a good job doesn't ensure that he'll have the same success next time. Seeing inconsistency in your players' technique can be frustrating. It's even more challenging to stay positive when your players repeatedly perform a skill incorrectly or have a lack of enthusiasm for learning. It can be quite frustrating to see players who seemingly don't heed your advice and continue to make the same mistakes.

Please know that it is normal to get frustrated sometimes when teaching skills. Nevertheless, part of successful coaching is controlling this frustration. Instead of getting upset, use these six guidelines for shaping skills:

1. *Think small initially.*

   Reward the first signs of behavior that approximate what you want. Then reward closer and closer approximations of the desired behavior. In short, use your reward power to shape the behavior you seek.

2. *Break skills into small steps.*

   For instance, in learning to dribble, one of your players does well in watching for defenders around the ball, but she's careless with dribbling the ball and doesn't effectively shield it from defenders. She often has the ball too far away from her as she dribbles, or she runs too fast and loses control of it. Reinforce the correct technique of watching for defenders and teach her how to keep the ball close. Once she masters these skills, focus on getting her to run at a speed at which she can control the ball.

3. *Develop one component of a skill at a time.*

   Don't try to shape two components of a skill at once. For example, in receiving a ball with the inside of the foot, players must first stop the ball and then control it by trapping it with the foot. Players should focus initially on one aspect (stopping the ball with the arch of the inside of the foot while cushioning it by pulling the receiving leg back slightly), and then on the other (controlling the ball by trapping it with the foot). When players have problems mastering a skill, it's often because they're trying to improve two or more components at once. Help these players to isolate a single component.

4. *Use reinforcement only occasionally, for the best examples.*

   By focusing only on the best examples, you will help players continue to improve once they've mastered the basics. Using occasional reinforcement during practice allows players to have more contact time with the ball rather than their having to constantly stop and listen to the coach. Soccer skills are best learned through a lot of random repetition, such as gamelike activities, and the coach needs to make the best use of team practice time by allowing the players as much time with the ball as possible.

5. *Relax your reward standards.*

   As players focus on mastering a new skill or attempt to integrate it with other skills, their old, well-learned skills may temporarily degenerate and you may need to relax your expectations. For example, a player who has learned how to receive a pass along the ground with the inside of the foot is now learning how to combine that skill with turning at the same time as he receives. While learning to combine the two skills and getting the timing down, he may have poor control of the ball. A similar degeneration of ball skills may occur during growth spurts while the coordination of muscles, tendons, and ligaments catches up to the growth of bones.

6. *Go back to the basics.*

   If, however, a well-learned skill degenerates for long, you may need to restore it by going back to the basics. If necessary, practice the skill using an activity in which the players have a larger practice area and less pressure from opponents so that they can relearn the skill.

> **Coaching Tip**
> Beginning with the U10 age group, coaches can ask players to self-coach. With the proper guidance and a positive team environment, young players can think about how they perform a skill and how they might be able to perform it better. Self-coaching is best done at practice, where a player can experiment with learning new skills.

Detecting and Correcting Errors

Good coaches recognize that players make two types of errors: learning errors and performance errors. Learning errors are ones that occur because players don't know how to perform a skill; that is, they have not yet developed the correct motor pattern in the brain to perform a particular skill. Players make performance errors not because they don't know how to execute the skill but because they have made a mistake in executing what they do know. There is no easy way to know whether a player is making learning or performance errors, and part of the art of coaching is being able to sort out which type of error each mistake is.

The process of helping players correct errors begins with your observing and evaluating their performances to determine whether the mistakes are learning or performance errors. Carefully watch your players to see whether they routinely make the errors in both practice and game settings, or whether the errors tend to occur only in game settings. If the latter is the case, then your players are making performance errors. For performance errors, you need to look for the reasons your players are not performing as well as they know how; perhaps they are nervous, or maybe they get distracted by the game setting. If the mistakes are learning errors, then you need to help them learn the skill, which is the focus of this section.

When correcting learning errors, there is no substitute for the coach knowing skills well. The better you understand a skill—not only how one performs it correctly but also what causes learning errors—the more helpful you will be in correcting mistakes.

One of the most common coaching mistakes is to provide inaccurate feedback and advice on how to correct errors. Don't rush into error correction; wrong feedback or poor advice will hurt the learning process more than no feedback or advice at all. If you are uncertain about the cause of the problem or how to correct it, continue to observe and analyze until you are more sure. As a rule, you should see the error repeated several times before attempting to correct it.

Correct One Error at a Time

Suppose Jill, one of your forwards, is having trouble with her shooting. She's doing most things well, but you notice that she's not keeping her foot pointed down as she strikes the ball, and she often approaches the ball sort of sideways, with her hips not square to the target. What do you do?

First, decide which error to begin with, because players learn more effectively when they attempt to correct one error at a time. Determine whether one error is causing the other; if so, have the player correct that error first, because it may eliminate the other error. In Jill's case, however, neither error is causing the other. In such cases, players should correct the error that is easiest to correct and that will bring the greatest improvement when remedied. For Jill, it probably means kicking with the toes of the kicking foot pointed down. Improving the kick will likely motivate her to correct the other error.

Use Positive Feedback to Correct Errors

The positive approach to correcting errors includes emphasizing what to do instead of what not to do. Use compliments, praise, rewards, and encouragement to correct errors. Acknowledge correct performance as well as efforts to improve. By using positive feedback, you can help your players feel good about themselves and promote a strong desire to achieve.

When you're working with one player at a time, the positive approach to correcting errors includes four steps:

1. *Praise effort and proper performance.*

   Praise the player for trying to perform a skill correctly and for performing any parts of it correctly. Do so immediately after he performs the skill, if possible. Keep the praise simple: "Good try," "Way to stay focused," "Good extension," or "That's the way to follow through." You can also use nonverbal feedback like smiling, clapping your hands, or any facial or body expression that shows approval.

   Make sure you're sincere with your praise. Don't indicate that a player's effort was good when it wasn't. Usually a player knows whether he has made a sincere effort to perform the skill correctly and perceives undeserved praise for what it is—untruthful feedback to make him feel good. Likewise, don't indicate that a player's performance was correct when it wasn't.

2. *Give simple and precise feedback to correct errors.*

   Don't burden a player with a long or detailed explanation of how to correct an error. Give just enough feedback that the player can correct one error at a time. Before giving feedback, recognize that some players readily accept it immediately after the error, whereas others respond better if you delay the correction slightly. Be brief while making your coaching point and get the player back into action quickly.

   For errors that are complicated to explain and difficult to correct, try the following:

   - Explain and demonstrate what the player should have done. Do not demonstrate what the player did wrong.
   - Explain the causes of the error, if they aren't obvious.
   - Explain why you are recommending the correction you have selected, if it's not obvious.

3. *Make sure the player understands your feedback.*

If the player doesn't understand your feedback, she won't be able to correct the error. Ask her to repeat the feedback and to explain and demonstrate how she will use it. If the player can't do this, be patient and present your feedback again. Then have her repeat the feedback after you're finished.

4. *Provide an environment that motivates the player to improve.*

Your players won't always be able to correct their errors immediately, even if they do understand your feedback. Encourage them to hang tough and stick with it when adjustments are difficult or when they seem discouraged. For more difficult corrections, remind them that it will take time, and that the improvement will happen only if they work at it. Encourage players who have little self-confidence. Saying something like this: "You were dribbling at a much better speed today; with practice, you'll be able to keep the ball closer to you and shield it from defenders." Such support can motivate a player to continue to refine his dribbling skills.

Other players may be very self-motivated and need little help from you in this area; with them you can practically ignore step 4 when correcting an error. Although motivation comes from within, try to provide an environment of positive instruction and encouragement to help your players improve.

A final note on correcting errors: Team sports such as soccer provide unique challenges in this endeavor. How do you provide individual feedback in a group setting using a positive approach? Instead of yelling across the field to correct an error (and embarrass the player), substitute for the player who erred. Then make the correction on the sidelines or during a subsequent practice session. This type of feedback has several advantages:

- The player will be more receptive to one-on-one feedback.
- The other players are active and still practicing skills, unable to hear your discussion.
- Because the rest of the team is still playing, you'll feel compelled to make your comments simple and concise, which is more helpful to the player.

This procedure doesn't mean you can't also use the team setting to give specific, positive feedback. You can do so to emphasize correct group and individual performances. Use this team feedback approach only for positive statements, though. Save corrections for individual discussion.

Dealing With Misbehavior

Children misbehave at times; it's only natural. Following are two ways you can respond to misbehavior, through extinction or discipline.

Extinction

Ignoring misbehavior—neither rewarding it nor disciplining it—is called extinction. This approach can be effective under certain circumstances. In some situations, disciplining young people's misbehavior only encourages them to act up further because of the recognition they get. Ignoring misbehavior teaches youngsters that it is not worth your attention.

Sometimes, though, you cannot wait for a behavior to fizzle out. When players cause danger to themselves or others or disrupt the activities of others, you need to take immediate action. Tell the offending player that the behavior must stop and that discipline will follow if it doesn't. If the child doesn't stop misbehaving after the warning, follow through with discipline.

Extinction also doesn't work well when misbehavior is self-rewarding. For example, you may be able to keep from grimacing if a youngster kicks you in the shin, but the kid still knows you were hurt—therein lies the reward. In such circumstances, you must discipline the player for the undesirable behavior.

Extinction works best in situations in which players are seeking recognition through mischievous behaviors, clowning, or grandstanding. Usually, if you are patient, their failure to get your attention will cause the behavior to disappear. However, be alert so that you don't extinguish desirable behavior. When youngsters do something well, they expect to be positively reinforced. Not rewarding them will likely cause them to discontinue the desired behavior.

Discipline

Some educators say we should never discipline young people but should only reinforce their positive behaviors. They argue that discipline does not work, creates hostility, and sometimes leads to avoidance behaviors that may be more unwholesome than the original problem behavior. It is true that discipline does not always work and that it can create problems when used ineffectively, but when used appropriately, discipline is effective in eliminating undesirable behaviors without creating undesirable consequences. You must use discipline effectively, because it is impossible to guide athletes through positive reinforcement and extinction alone. Discipline is part of the positive approach when these guidelines are followed:

- Discipline in a corrective way to help players improve now and in the future. Don't discipline to retaliate and make yourself feel better.

- Impose discipline in a matter-of-fact way when players break team rules or otherwise misbehave. Shouting at or scolding children indicates that your attitude is one of revenge.
- Once a good rule has been agreed on, ensure that players who violate it experience the unpleasant consequences of their misbehavior. Warn players once before disciplining, but don't wave discipline threateningly over their heads—just do it.
- Be consistent in administering discipline.
- Don't discipline using consequences that may cause you guilt. If you can't think of an appropriate consequence right away, tell the player you will talk with her after you think about it. You might consider involving the player in designing a consequence.
- Once the discipline is completed, don't make players feel that they are in the doghouse. Always let them know that they're valued members of the team.
- Make sure that what you think is discipline isn't perceived by the player as a positive reinforcement. For instance, keeping a player out of a certain activity or portion of the training session may be just what the child desired.
- Never discipline players for making errors when they are playing.
- Never use physical activity—running laps or doing push-ups—as discipline. To do so only causes players to resent physical activity, whereas we want them to learn to enjoy it throughout their lives.
- Discipline sparingly. Constant discipline and criticism cause players to resent you and to turn their interests elsewhere as well.

7

Coaching Offense

This chapter focuses on the offensive techniques and tactics your players must learn in order to perform effectively in youth soccer games. Remember to use the IDEA approach to teaching skills: introduce, demonstrate, and explain the skill, and then attend to players as they practice it (see page 54 in chapter 6). This chapter also ties in directly to the season and practice plans in chapter 10. It describes the technical and tactical skills that you'll teach at the practices outlined there. If you aren't familiar with soccer skills, rent or purchase a video so that you can see the skills performed correctly. Also, the Coaching Youth Soccer online course offered by ASEP and US Youth Soccer can help you further understand these skills (you can take this course by going to www.asep.com).

Because the information in this book is limited to soccer basics, you will need to advance your coaching knowledge as your players advance their skills. You can do this by learning from your experiences, watching and talking with more experienced coaches, attending coaching courses conducted by your state association, and studying resources on advanced skills.

Offensive Technical Skills

The offensive skills that you will teach your players are dribbling, passing, receiving, heading, and shooting. Mastering these techniques will enable your players to better execute your offensive tactics—or set plays—during a game. These basic skills serve as the foundation for playing soccer well at all levels. Soccer players practice these technical skills at every practice, from youth soccer to the pros.

Dribbling

Dribbling is moving and controlling the ball using only the feet. Soccer players dribble to move the ball down the field for a pass or shot, to keep the ball from the opposing team, and to change direction. Some players may have trouble dribbling at first, especially those at younger levels or those who have not played soccer before.

Players need to be able to use the inside and outside of each foot as well as the sole and the instep to dribble, while keeping the ball near the body and close to the feet (see figure 7.1). When dribbling with the inside of the foot, the player turns the foot out and then pushes the ball forward with the arch of the foot. When dribbling with the outside of the foot, the player turns the foot in and then pushes the ball slightly forward or to the side with the side of the foot.

Coaching Tip

Encourage players to use either foot to dribble, because this versatility will make it easier for them to protect the ball from opponents. The ability to change speed and direction with either foot will greatly advance the player's skills.

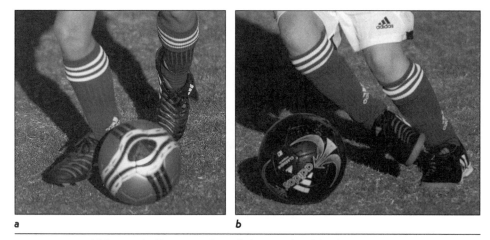

Figure 7.1   Dribbling with the *(a)* inside and *(b)* outside of the foot.

Players should first practice dribbling at a slow pace, such as dribbling while walking. Once they can do so and feel more comfortable with the technique, they can speed up their pace. As your players improve, you can have them dribble against an opponent to help teach them other important aspects of the technique of dribbling, such as varying their speed, changing direction, and shielding the ball. You can also help prepare them for defensive pressure by practicing speeding up and slowing down as they dribble or dribbling around cones or other objects.

Use these points to teach your players how to dribble correctly:

- Push the ball softly in the desired direction, especially if you are dribbling close to defenders.
- Don't constantly watch the ball. Learn to glance up and down at the ball in order to control it and at the same time scan the field. When you are always looking down, an opponent is more likely to be able to steal the ball, or you may not see another teammate who is open for a pass.
- Shield the ball from opponents by positioning your body between the ball and the opponent.
- Move at a speed at which you can control the ball.

It is common for the ball to get away from players at younger levels because their eye and foot coordination, balance, and control of the force with which they touch the ball are not fully developed. A deft touch on the ball comes only with age and years of practice. When the ball gets away, players run the risk of it being stolen by the opponent. To help your players control the ball while dribbling, teach them the following:

- Keep the ball near the body, close to the feet, as shown in figure 7.1.
- Nudge the ball gently in different directions, never letting it get more than a stride's length away.

For the older age groups, preferably U8 and up, intentional speed dribbling—dribbling at a high speed—is acceptable. Speed dribbling is done by pushing the ball out several feet ahead and then sprinting to the ball. When dribbling at high speeds, however, players must keep a close eye out for the opponents and for open teammates. Above all, they must keep their heads up.

Dribbling Touch

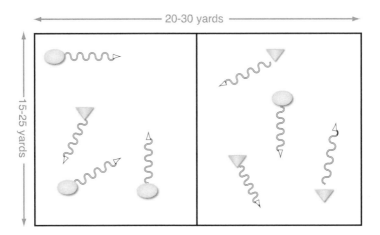

Players divide into two teams, and each team positions in one-half of the playing area as shown in the diagram. Each player has a ball; one player from each team acts as a tagger and plays in the other team's half. All players dribble in their area while the tagger attempts to tag as many players as possible without losing control of the ball. The coach names a new tagger after a specified amount of playing time. The new tagger enters the other team's area to replace the previous tagger, and play continues. Two games can be set up simultaneously in order to involve all of the players on the team.

- *U6:* Players divide into two teams of 3 players each and position in a 20-by-15-yard playing area; 1-minute playing time.
- *U8:* Players divide into two teams of 4 players each and position in a 20-by-15-yard playing area; 1-minute playing time.
- *U10:* Players divide into two teams of 6 players each and position in a 25-by-20-yard playing area; 2-minute playing time.
- *U12:* Players divide into two teams of 8 players each and position in a 25-by-20-yard playing area; 2-minute playing time.
- *U14:* Players divide into two teams of 8 players each and position in a 30-by-25-yard playing area; 3-minute playing time.

Passing

Passing is the invisible thread that ties teammates together. Passing allows a team to maintain possession of the ball and create scoring opportunities or penetrate toward the opposing goal. Passes should be accurate, with appropriate pace, and players should release them with proper timing and disguise. Inaccurate or slow passes are likely to be stolen by an opposing player. The length of the pass will vary according to the tactical circumstances, such as where the player with the ball is positioned and where teammates are positioned. Here we will discuss two of the more common types of passes—short and long.

Short Passes

Players use short passes (or push passes) most often, because of their accuracy. It is best to use the push pass when the receiver is within 20 yards of the passer. Of course, the passing distance of younger players will be shorter, whereas older players may be able to pass farther on their so-called short passes. Use these points to teach your players how to make a short pass:

- Plant the nonkicking foot alongside and near the ball (see figure 7.2*a*).
- Square up the hips and shoulders to the receiver and turn out the kicking foot (see figure 7.2*b*).
- Swing the kicking foot straight at the center of the ball.
- Follow through by swinging the kicking leg well beyond the point of impact with the ball, in the direction of the receiver (see figure 7.2*c*).

a   b   c

Figure 7.2 (a-c)   Short pass.

Tiger Ball

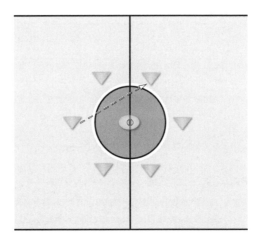

Players position around the center circle with one player inside the circle, as shown in the diagram. Players positioned around the circle pass the ball to each other while the player inside the circle attempts to intercept the passes. The ball may be passed in any direction. If the player in the circle touches the ball, if the passer uses any part of the foot besides the inside to pass, or if the ball goes above head height, the inside player switches positions with the player who last passed the ball and play continues.

- *U6:* Use 4 players positioned around the center circle; 30-second playing time.
- *U8:* Use 4 players positioned around the center circle; 1-minute playing time.
- *U10:* Use 6 players positioned around the center circle; 1-minute playing time.
- *U12:* Use 6 players positioned around the center circle; 1-minute playing time. Use activity to practice first-touch passing.
- *U14:* Use 6 players positioned around the center circle; 2-minute playing time. Use the activity to practice first-touch passing.

Long Passes

Long passes are made when a game situation calls for a player to make a long pass to a teammate across the field. The long pass can be either on the ground or in the air, but it is generally best to do it in the air because it is less likely to be intercepted by an opponent. Use these points to teach your players how to make a long pass:

- Plant the nonkicking foot slightly behind and to the side of the ball, with the toes pointing toward the receiver (see figure 7.3a).
- Square up the hips and shoulders to the receiver.

- Point the toes of the kicking foot down and kick underneath the ball with the top of the foot, at the shoelace or instep area.

- Watch the kicking foot as it contacts the bottom half of the ball (or the middle of the ball for a long pass along the ground) and lifts it off the ground. Keep the kicking foot firm throughout the kicking motion (see figure 7.3*b*).

- Follow through by swinging the kicking leg slightly up and across the body (see figure 7.3*c*).

a   b   c

Figure 7.3 (a-c)   Long pass.

First-Touch Passes

A first-touch pass can be a long or short pass that a player makes with his first touch of the ball. This pass requires experienced ability to read the movement of the ball, in order for the player to get his body into the correct position to make a pass on the first touch. Players may call on such passes when opponents are tightly marking them or when they are about to receive a ball that is in danger of being taken by an opponent. Passing technique is essentially the same as that described for both the short and long passes, depending on the distance of the pass. This pass is possible in the U8 and U10 age groups, but players in the U12 age group and up are likely to perform it with greater consistency. Coaches of U8 and U10 players do better to teach their youngsters to receive, control, and then pass the ball, using two or three touches of the ball.

Kicking for Distance

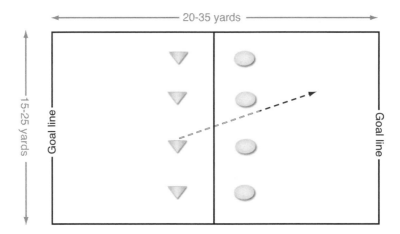

Players divide into two teams and position at an equal distance on either side of the playing area's center line, as shown in the diagram. A player on one team starts play by making a long pass as far as she can toward the opposing goal line, in an attempt to drive the opposing team back to their goal line. The opposing team must allow the ball to land and then play it from that spot back into the other half.

- *U6:* The activity is inappropriate for this age group.
- *U8:* Players divide into two teams of 4 players each and position in a 20-by-15-yard playing area; 5-minute playing time.
- *U10:* Players divide into two teams of 6 players each and position in a 25-by-20-yard playing area; 5-minute playing time.
- *U12:* Players divide into two teams of 6 players each and position in a 30-by-25-yard playing area; 5-minute playing time. If necessary, use two grids to involve all of the players.
- *U14:* Players divide into two teams of 6 players each and position in a 35-by-25-yard playing area; 5-minute playing time. If necessary, use two grids to involve all of the players.

Receiving

Controlling and moving a passed ball all in one motion is called receiving. A player may receive the ball with just about any part of the body—the foot, the thigh, or the chest.

Receiving With the Foot

A ball is typically received with the foot when the ball is approaching a player on the ground. The U8 age group and up, however, can also use the foot to receive a bouncing ball. The U10 age group and up can use the foot to receive a ball in the air. Receiving a ball that is on or near the ground with the inside of the foot provides the most surface area; it is the best method for younger or inexperienced players. Properly receiving a ball on or near the ground, however, is all about knowing how to cushion the ball. If a player does not cushion the ball, it will bounce away from the foot and the player will lose control. Use these points to teach players how to receive a ball with the inside of the foot:

- Stand in front of the ball and extend a leg and foot out to meet it (see figure 7.4a).
- Contact the bottom and side of the ball with the inside of the foot, midway between the heel and toes, and cushion the impact of the ball by relaxing the foot as the ball contacts it (see figure 7.4b).
- Pull the leg back to slow the ball (see figure 7.4c).

Coaching Tip
Correct execution of the skill of receiving is possible for the U10 age group and up. For the U6 age group, coaches should focus on teaching players the mechanics of just stopping the ball. At the U8 age level, coaches can begin teaching players the concept of trapping—stopping the ball while in a stationary position—and can also begin occasionally experimenting with receiving.

a   b   c

Figure 7.4 (a-c) Receiving with the inside of the foot.

Players should also learn how to receive with the outside and top of both feet, because players will not always be in a position to receive the ball with the inside of the foot. For example, a player may choose to use the outside of the foot to receive the ball if he is being marked by an opponent, because doing so can help to shield the ball from the opponent. Receiving with the outside of the foot, as shown in figure 7.5, is the same as receiving with the inside of the foot except that the contact surface is smaller. Mistakes, however, may be more likely to occur while players learn the proper touch to control the ball with the outside of the foot. Receiving with the top of the foot, as shown in figure 7.6, requires the player to first accurately judge the flight of the ball, but the procedure is then the same as receiving with the inside of the foot.

Coaching Tip

Receiving a ball from the air with any part of the foot is a skill best taught to the U12 age group and up. Children generally do not develop enough visual acuity to properly judge the flight of a ball in the air until around age 10, so for the U10 age group and younger, coaches should focus on receiving ground balls and bouncing balls.

Figure 7.5   Receiving with the outside of the foot.

Figure 7.6   Receiving with the top of the foot.

Horseshoes

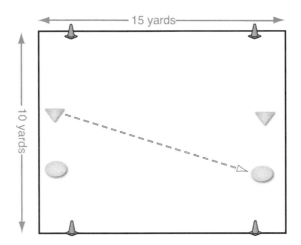

Players divide into two teams with players from each team positioned at each end of the playing area, as shown in the diagram. Cones are placed one yard from the end line on each end. To begin, a player on one team makes a pass to a player on the opposing team who is positioned at the opposite end of the area. This second player attempts to receive the ball and stop it as close to the cone as possible. The player then plays the ball back to another player on the other team, where this opposing player also attempts to receive and control the pass.

- *U6:* Players divide into two teams of 2 players each and position in a 15-by-10-yard playing area; 30-second playing time. All passes should be on the ground.

- *U8:* Players divide into two teams of 4 players each and position in a 15-by-10-yard playing area; 1-minute playing time. All passes should be on the ground.

- *U10:* Players divide into two teams of 4 players each and position in a 15-by-10-yard playing area; 2-minute playing time. All passes should be on the ground.

- *U12:* Players divide into two teams of 4 players each and position in a 15-by-10-yard playing area; 5-minute playing time. Passes may be on the ground or in the air.

- *U14:* Players divide into two teams of 4 players each and position in a 15-by-10-yard playing area; 5-minute playing time. Passes may be on the ground or in the air.

Receiving With the Thigh

A ball is typically received with the thigh when it approaches a player from the air. Use these points to teach your players how to receive a ball with the thigh:

- Stand in front of the ball and flex one knee (see figure 7.7a).
- Raise the leg so that the thigh is parallel to the ground and in line with the descent of the ball (see figure 7.7b).
- Stop the ball, cushioning it by dropping the knee slightly as the ball touches the midthigh halfway between the knee and the hip (see figure 7.7c).
- As the ball drops to the ground, control the ball by trapping it with the foot (see figure 7.7d).

a

b

c

d

Figure 7.7 (a-d)   Receiving with the thigh.

Thighs

Players divide into pairs and position 5-10 yards apart, facing each other. One player (server) tosses the ball underhand to the other player (receiver), who controls the ball with his thigh. The receiver then lets the ball drop to the ground and passes the ball back to the server. The server repeats the underhand toss, and the receiver must use the opposite thigh. Players switch roles after a set number of repetitions. They should remain stationary when starting this activity and progress to receiving with the thigh while on the move.

- *U6 and U8:* The activity is inappropriate for these age groups.
- *U10-U14:* Do 10 repetitions (5 with each thigh).

Receiving With the Chest

A ball is typically received with the chest when it approaches a player from the air. Use these points to teach your players how to receive a ball with the chest:

- Stand in the line of flight of the ball, with arms held up for balance and chest pushed out to meet the ball (see figure 7.8*a*).
- Allow the ball to make contact just right or left of center chest, where muscle and soft tissue provide an excellent receiving surface.
- As the ball contacts the body, exhale to relax the controlling surface and pull the chest back a few inches to cushion the ball (see figure 7.8*b*).
- As the ball drops to the ground, control the ball by trapping it with the foot (see figure 7.8*c*).

a   b   c

Figure 7.8 (a-c)   Receiving with the chest.

Windows

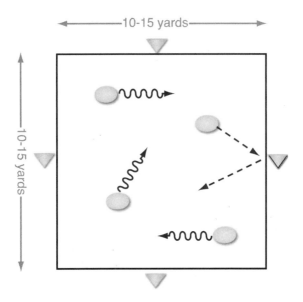

Players divide into two teams with players positioned on the outside and inside of the playing area, as shown in the diagram. The players on the inside of the playing area each dribble a ball and pass occasionally to a player on the outside of the playing area. When an outside player receives a ball, this outside player must then make a return pass, anywhere in the area, for the player on the inside to receive.

- *U6 and U8:* Players divide into two teams of 4 players each and position in a 10-by-10-yard playing area; 30-seconds playing time. All passes should be on the ground, and players on the outside can take as many touches as necessary to control the ball and return the pass.

- *U10:* Players divide into two teams of 4 players each and position in a 15-by-15-yard playing area; 1-minute playing time. Passes should stay on the ground or bounce. Players on the outside play two-touch to control the ball and return the pass.

- *U12 and U14:* Players divide into two teams of 4 players each and position in a 15-by-15-yard playing area; 2-minute playing time. Passes may remain on the ground, bounce, or go in the air. Players on the outside play one-touch to control the ball and return the pass.

Heading

Your players can clear a ball from an area of attack using a skill called heading, which is the technique of using the forehead, between the eyebrows and the hairline, to propel and direct the ball. Use these points to teach your players how to head the ball:

- Assume a balanced and relaxed stance with the feet slightly apart. Pull the head and body back and move to the ball (see figure 7.9a).
- Thrust the body forward to meet the ball, hitting it with the forehead at the hairline (see figure 7.9b).
- Clench the neck muscles, keeping the neck firm while driving forward (see figure 7.9c).

a   b   c

Figure 7.9 (a-c)   Heading the ball.

Heading is often performed incorrectly because coaches often don't know the exact technique involved. Beginning players and coaches can better learn this skill using an underinflated or foam soccer ball to practice individual juggling with the head. This exercise helps players be sure the ball contacts the correct part of the forehead and allows them more practice at judging the movement of the ball in the air.

Head Start

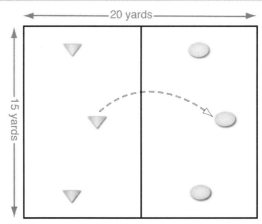

U12 and U14 players divide into two teams of 3 players, and each team positions anywhere in half of a 20-by-15-yard playing area, as shown in the diagram. Players may move anywhere in their half at any time. One team begins, with one player heading the ball into the other half from behind the halfway line. The players on the other team attempt to catch the ball in the air. If the ball is caught, the catcher may take one step forward and head the ball back. Otherwise, the ball is headed from the spot where it lands. The teams continue to head the ball, attempting to force their opponents back and move themselves forward. Direct returns are allowed. If the ball goes out of bounds, the game is resumed with a throw-in, and the ball should be headed from the throw-in.

Shooting

Nothing puts greater pressure on the defense than shots on goal, so your players should become comfortable with the skill of shooting.

A good shot has the same qualities as a good pass—accuracy, proper pace, and timing. So when you first teach the skill of shooting, you may want to point out the similarities. For example, shots also come from the inside, instep, and outside of the foot. Also mention some of these key differences between shooting and passing:

- Length—Shots often must travel a greater distance than passes, because defenders work to keep offensive players away from the goal.

- Speed—Shooters frequently kick the ball harder than passers do so that the keeper can't react to stop the shot. Unlike the passer, the shooter doesn't need to be concerned about whether a teammate can control the kick.

- Purpose—Shots are taken for one reason: to score a goal. However, players pass the ball for many different reasons, such as to get a better shot or to keep the ball away from the defense.

Use these points to teach your players how to shoot a ball:

- Approach the ball from behind and at a slight angle, with the shoulders and hips square to the target. Keep the head steady and the eyes focused on the ball (see figure 7.10a-b).

- Take a long step to help draw the kicking leg back and plant the balance foot beside the ball, with the knee slightly flexed. Keep the kicking leg cocked until the nonkicking foot is firmly planted beside the ball (see figure 7.10c).

- Extend the kicking foot, keeping the knee of the kicking leg directly over the ball.

- Whip the kicking leg straight and contact the center of the ball with the instep. Keep the foot firm as it strikes the ball and the toes pointed down.

- Follow through completely, keeping the kicking leg pointing toward the goal well beyond the point of impact (see figure 7.10d).

Coaching Tip

Older or more accurate shooters should aim away from the keeper and toward the corners of the goal. Younger or less accurate shooters can also attempt to hit the corners but might consider using the whole goal as the target at times. Once a goalkeeper becomes part of the game, shooting requires greater accuracy; in order to beat the goalkeeper, the best spot to place a shot is in the corners of the goal.

a

b

c

d

Figure 7.10 (a-d) Shooting the ball.

Hot Shots

Players divide into two teams of 4 players and position on half of the field. A half circle is marked in front of the goal, as shown in the diagram. The game is started by a neutral goal kick made by a player designated by the coach. One team attacks, trying to score goals, while the other plays defense to avoid conceding them. A goal may be scored only by a shot from outside the circle. If a player treads within the circle, the other team is awarded a direct free kick from that spot—no offside or corner kicks. Balls that roll into the shooting circle either go to the goalkeeper (U10 and up) or go back into play with a kick-in (U6 and U8). All balls that go out of bounds are brought back into play with a throw-in (U8-U14) or a kick-in (U6).

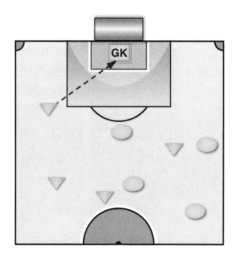

- *U6:* Players divide into two teams of 4 players and position on half of the field (30 by 25 yards) with a 6-by-18-yard or smaller goal size; 5-minute playing time.
- *U8:* Players divide into two teams of 4 players and position on half of the field (35 by 30 yards) with a 6-by-18-yard or smaller goal size; 5- to 7-minute playing time.
- *U10:* Players divide into two teams of 4 players and position on half of the field (60 by 45 yards) with a 6-by-18-yard goal size. Add a neutral goalkeeper; 10-minute playing time.
- *U12:* Players divide into two teams of 4 players and position on half of the field (80 by 55 yards) with a 6-by-18-yard goal size. Add a neutral goalkeeper; 15-minute playing time.
- *U14:* Players divide into two teams of 4 players and position on half of the field (105 by 65 yards) with an 8-by-24-yard goal size. Add a neutral goalkeeper; 15-minute playing time.

Offensive Set Play Techniques

Players need repeated practice to master the basic skills of soccer, but they must also learn how to use these skills in game situations. Some of those situations are set plays requiring good passing, shooting, and perhaps, heading skills.

Corner Kick

A corner kick is a direct free kick taken by the offense if the ball goes out of bounds across the goal line when it was last touched by the defense. Corner kicks are taken from the corner arc and are executed most successfully when they are initiated by a kicker who can deliver an accurate pass to either the near post area or far post area. For a corner kick, kickers typically use an instep drive, which is a powerful kick made with the top of the foot. The best kicks are hard, low kicks across the face of the goal; these kicks should be in the air, not on the ground. Higher, softer kicks—and kicks on the ground—are easier to defend. Hard, low balls across the face of the goal present more opportunities for the attackers.

Goal Kick

A goal kick is a placekick made by the defense if the ball goes out of bounds across the goal line when it was last touched by the offense. The goal kick is taken from the goal area. The kicker, usually the goalkeeper, places the plant foot beside the ball (approximately 4 inches to the side) with the toes pointing toward the target and the knee of the standing leg slightly bent. The kicking leg swings back and then forward to strike the ball, with the toes of the kicking foot pointed down, the ankle locked, and the knee slightly bent. The knuckle of the big toe should go under the ball to provide a slight lift to the pass, and the instep should drive through the ball to provide distance to the pass. Players should lean slightly forward when making this kick and keep their eyes on the ball to ensure proper contact. Players should not bring their heads up until the follow-through of the kicking leg is complete.

Penalty Kick

A penalty kick is a direct free kick awarded to the offense when the defense commits a major offense within their own penalty area. For the penalty kick, most shooters try to place the ball in a corner of the goal and use an instep drive or push pass to do so. The instep drive provides the power needed to beat the goalkeeper, and it may be necessary against older and faster goalkeepers. The push pass is highly accurate but slower, and a goalkeeper with good reaction speed may be more likely to make the save. Players should also be aware that low shots work best to beat the goalkeeper.

Offensive Tactical Skills

Once your team can understand and properly execute the individual offensive technical skills, they can begin putting them together into offensive schemes, or tactics. The tactics you should teach your players to use when your team has the ball are providing support, moving continuously, spreading out the attack, and improvising in the attacking half of the field.

Providing Support

Essential to any soccer team's offensive success is how players support their teammates on the field. The triangle formation, as shown in figure 7.11, is a way you can reinforce to players in the U10 age group and up the need to provide support to spread out the defense. The triangle formation helps to give the player with the ball more options, such as continuing to dribble, making a pass, or shooting on goal if space is opened up by teammates off the ball. It also provides for width and depth, which are other important principles of attack.

> **Coaching Tip**
>
> A simple way to teach the proper triangle formation positioning to players in the U10 age group and up is to position players along the outer edges of the dribbler's field of vision. This outer edge can be found by swinging both arms from behind the back around to the front until they are just visible.

The triangle formation is used in sports such as hockey and basketball in which a fluid, dynamic interplay is required. To achieve this formation, players in the immediate vicinity of the ball should work to maintain triangle positioning on the field, with the dribbler usually at the apex of the triangle. In other words, only two or three players should provide support at one time, because more will draw too many defenders and clog the attack. Players should attempt to maintain a

Figure 7.11   Triangle formation.

3- to 5-yard distance from the ball when in close quarters and an 8- to 10-yard distance if defenders are not challenging for possession.

Additionally, coaches of the U12 age group and up should teach players the concept of maintaining a diamond formation in the vicinity of the ball when attacking (see figure 7.12). This shape provides more depth and width simultaneously and creates more options for the teammate in possession of the ball.

Coaches should keep in mind that for the U6 age group, the focus should be on creating individual solutions to the game's challenges; therefore, they should not introduce the triangle concept at this young age. The U8 age group will also be individually oriented for the most part, but they should be capable of working in pairs.

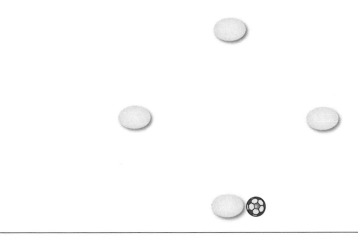

Figure 7.12   Diamond formation.

Wall Passes

The wall pass, or give-and-go, is an advanced support skill in which two attackers can work together to beat a single defender.

To execute the wall pass, the player with the ball dribbles at the defending player, committing the defender to her, then passes to a nearby teammate before sprinting into the space behind the defender to collect a return pass. Note that to commit a defender to her, the attacker must get the defender to step forward to tackle the ball.

It is the dribbler's responsibility to engage the defender and then to successfully pass to the support attacker. It is the support attacker's responsibility to be about three to four yards to the side of the defending player, at about a 45-degree angle from the dribbler. The support attacker executes a one-touch pass to the space behind the defender and then sprints forward to support her teammate.

Moving Continuously

Offensive players are easy to mark if they are inactive, so you must encourage your players to move continuously to an open area to receive passes from teammates. The dribbler should keep this principle in mind as well; if other players are not open, he should also strive to move the ball to an open area. This tactic will put pressure on the defense and most likely will cause one of the defensive players to leave his player, thus leaving an offensive player open for a pass. However, players should not run merely for the sake of running. Offensive off-the-ball runs need to be for a tactical purpose, such as to support the teammate in possession of the ball, to create space for that player, or to create space for himself. As discussed in the previous section, attackers at the U10 age group and up should also strive to maintain the triangle shape around the ball.

Additionally, when a pass is made, the player for whom the pass is intended should move to meet the ball as quickly as possible while still maintaining sufficient control to receive the pass. Players must be aware of the pass, including its direction and velocity, and must pay particular attention to the position of defenders in relation to the path of the pass. Moving to meet the ball makes it less likely that the pass will be intercepted by the opposition.

Spreading Out the Attack

Your players should strive to keep appropriate distances between each other on the field. By spreading your attack, your team can open up space for dribbling, passing, and scoring opportunities. There is no tactical difference between spreading out the attack and providing support, as discussed previously on page 84. The players in the diamond or triangle formations are considered support near the vicinity of the ball. When players spread out the attack, however, those farther from the ball also provide support. This concept becomes important for the U12 age group and up—since they will be able to pass the ball farther, the tactical idea of spreading out becomes more real to them. Because of less strength, unrefined technique, and tactical immaturity, the U10 and younger age groups will not play the ball over such large distances; they generally play the game within close vicinity of the ball.

Passing and Shooting Frequently

Quick, frequent passes require the defense to adjust constantly. Also, when defenders are out of position, openings are created for shots on goal. The more shots on goal taken by your players from reasonable distances and angles, the greater your team's chances to score.

Coaches should keep in mind that the U6 and U8 age groups typically will not pass with intentional forethought or will be inconsistent in their passing. The U10 age group and up will regularly pass on purpose. The older the players, the more often passing—leading to shots on goal—will occur.

8

Coaching Defense

Playing defense consists largely of instinct and effort, but practice and repetition will help improve your players' defensive techniques and tactics. This chapter focuses on the defensive techniques and tactics that your players must learn to succeed in youth soccer.

Defensive Technical Skills

The five defensive technical skills your players need to learn are marking, tackling, heading, intercepting passes, and making clearances.

Marking

Marking is the skill of guarding offensive players to prevent them from scoring. The defense uses it to slow down an opponent and to allow teammates to recover to their positions. Marking is a good example of the link between technique and tactics. Selecting whom to mark, (and when, where, and for how long), is primarily a player's tactical decision. From a technical viewpoint, however, marking an opponent well requires correct physical positioning and posture.

Defenders should try to mark the offensive player nearest them by positioning themselves between that player and the goal, which is called being "goalside." For example, in figure 8.1, player A is goalside of player B. From this position, defensive players are better able to gain possession of the ball off the dribble and to intercept passes. Also, the closer a defender is to the player with the ball, the more difficult it is for that player to pass, dribble, or shoot. So marking gives defensive players a better chance of stealing or blocking the ball when the opponent passes or shoots.

Use these points when teaching your players how to mark:

- Maintain ready position with feet slightly less than shoulder-width apart, knees bent, and body leaning slightly forward. The head should be steady and the arms slightly out to help maintain balance.

- Eyes should be focused on the ball and on the dribbler's hips.

- Adjust positioning based on the dribbler's speed, ability, and location on the field.

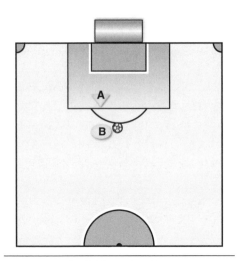

Figure 8.1   Goalside positioning.

Marking Man

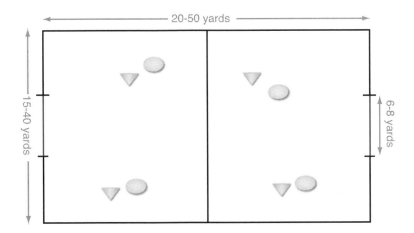

Players divide into two teams and position in a playing area, divided by a halfway line and with goals set up at each end, as shown in the diagram. No goalkeepers are used. Each defensive player is assigned a specific opponent to mark, which is known as man-to-man marking. The offense attempts to score while the defense attempts to prevent goals by using effective marking. The game starts when the defense passes the ball across the halfway line to the attack. Defensive players may tackle only their own offensive player; help from teammates is not allowed. The offensive players keep the ball if they beat the player marking them in the tackle, after a goal, or after fouls, or if the ball goes out of bounds. No player may cross the halfway line.

- *U6:* The activity is not appropriate for this age group.
- *U8:* Players divide into two teams of 3 to 4 players each and position in a 20-by-15-yard playing area with 6-yard-wide goals; 10-minute playing time.
- *U10:* Players divide into two teams of 4 players each and position in a 30-by-20-yard playing area with 6-yard-wide goals; 10- to 15-minute playing time.
- *U12:* Players divide into two teams of 4 to 6 players each and position in a 30-by-20-yard to 40-by-30-yard playing area with 6-yard-wide goals; 15-minute playing time.
- *U14:* Players divide into two teams of 5 to 7 players each and position in a 40-by-30-yard to 50-by-40-yard playing area with 8-yard-wide goals; 20-minute playing time.

Tackling

Taking the ball from an offensive player is called tackling. The primary intent of tackling is for the tackler to gain possession of the ball. To simply kick the ball away from the dribbler may dispossess the attacker but does not gain possession for the tackler. Effective tackling is all about timing. Ideally, your players should step in whenever the attacker temporarily loses control of the ball. Players should not be afraid to attempt to take the ball when they have a good opportunity, such as when the dribbler pushes the ball too far ahead or when a player does not receive a pass correctly.

Lunging at the ball—also called diving in—is a poor tactic for gaining possession, and a good dribbler usually goes around a defender who does so, with no trouble. Also, the Laws of the Game require the tackler to contact the ball before the opponent and to intentionally play the ball—not rush the opponent, which would be an unfair charge and warrants a foul. When positioning to make a tackle, the defender should instead approach the dribbler in a sideways position and should go for the ball, not the dribbler (see figure 8.2). If the defender follows this technique, the attacker cannot push the ball between the defender's legs. Defenders should also, however, be prepared to reestablish a good defensive position if they are unsuccessful in their tackling attempts.

Your players can use two types of tackles, depending on the situation they are in. These are the block tackle and the poke tackle.

> **Coaching Tip**
>
> Teach players in the U10 age group and up to pay close attention to an opponent's habits, such as using only one foot to dribble, pass, or shoot. Then, if these habits occur during the flow of play, they'll be able to outwit the offensive players and perhaps block or gain possession of the ball more frequently.

Figure 8.2   Approaching the tackle in a sideways position.

Block Tackle for Possession

Your players will want to use a block tackle when an opponent is dribbling directly at them, because the tactical objective is to gain possession of the ball for the tackler's team. The block is the most common type of tackle in soccer, and this technique is the foundation of skillful defending.

Use the following points to teach your players how to block tackle:

- Quickly close the distance between yourself and the dribbler.
- Assume a slightly crouched position, with the feet in a staggered stance in order to react more quickly to the dribbler's move (see figure 8.3*a*).
- To make the tackle, position the foot sideways, making contact with the inside surface of the foot. The foot must be kept firm as it drives into the ball (see figure 8.3*b*).

a   b

Figure 8.3 (a-b)   Block tackle.

Poke Tackle to Dispossess

Your players can use a poke tackle when they are approaching an opponent from the side or from slightly behind. Whereas the block tackle is used for the primary intent of tackling, to gain possession, the poke tackle is used to achieve the secondary intent of tackling, which is to dispossess the opponent.

Use the following points to teach your players how to poke tackle:

- Mark the dribbler as previously specified and watch for an opportunity to attack the ball.
- Move near the dribbler and plant the nonkicking foot away from the ball (see figure 8.4*a*).
- With the toes of the other foot, use a short, firm kick near the center of the ball to knock it away from the opponent (see figure 8.4*b*).

a

b

Figure 8.4 (a-b)   Poke tackle.

Double Zone

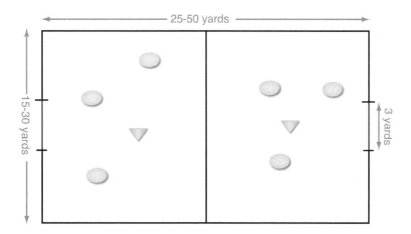

Players divide into two teams and position in a playing area with 3-yard-wide goals set up on the goal line (corner flags or tall cones can be used), as shown in the diagram. Each team has both attackers and defenders. The attackers try to score goals, and the defenders try to stop them. For both teams, attackers are positioned in the opposing half of the playing area and defenders are positioned in their own half. The coach should have all of the balls just off the field at the point where the halfway line meets the touchline. The game starts with a kick-in from the coach, who may also put a spare ball into play as needed. No player may cross over the halfway line. If the defense wins the ball from the attackers, if the ball goes out of play, or if there is an infringement of the rules, the other attackers get the ball. Attackers and defenders must change positions at regular intervals.

- *U6:* The activity is not appropriate for this age group.
- *U8:* Players divide into two teams of 4 players each (3 attackers and 1 defender) and position in a 25-by-15-yard playing area with a 3-yard-wide goal; 10-minute playing time.
- *U10 and U12:* Players divide into two teams of 5 players each (3 attackers and 2 defenders) and position in a 40-by-20-yard playing area with a 3-yard-wide goal; 15-minute playing time.
- *U14:* Players divide into two teams of 5 players each (3 attackers and 2 defenders) and position in a 50-by-30-yard playing area with a 3-yard-wide goal; 20-minute playing time.

Heading

When playing on defense, players use the skill of heading to clear the ball away from scoring range of the goal. The need to head the ball usually arises from a crossed ball or the opposing goalkeeper's punt. The technical aspects of heading the ball, however, are basically the same whether playing on offense or defense, except that players on defense should strike the ball on the bottom half in order to send it high over attackers. The primary goal of heading to clear the ball when on defense is to get the ball away from the danger zone (see figure 8.5).

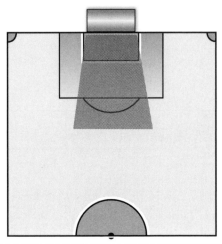

Figure 8.5   Danger zone.

Intercepting Passes

Players on the defending team should try to intercept a pass whenever possible, rather than waiting for an attacker to receive the pass before they attempt to regain possession of the ball. Starting a counterattack off an intercepted pass is much easier than starting it after a tackle or after a regain of possession from a ball played out of bounds. Defenders need to be alert for opportunities to intercept passes. Intercepting, which is stepping in between the receiver and the ball before the receiver can get it, requires good timing. The best time to intercept a pass is when the receiver is stationary and the pass is slow.

Following are cues for defenders to ask themselves when looking for the best interception opportunities. If the answers are yes to all, then the opportunity is probably a good one.

- Are the receiver's feet flat?
- Is the receiver not moving to the pass or moving slowly?
- Is the receiver looking only at the ball, not aware of defenders around her?

The mechanics of intercepting the ball are the same as those of receiving it. The defender who intercepts the ball then becomes the receiver.

Interception

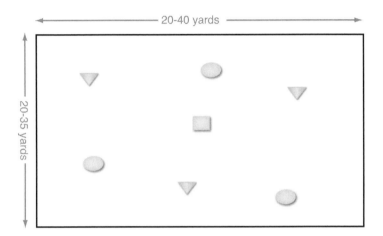

Players divide into two teams and position in a playing area as shown in the diagram. One neutral player, also positioned in the playing area, will start play by passing to a player on either team. The player who receives the ball will pass to another teammate and the team will make passes amongst themselves. The opposing team will look for opportunities to block or steal passes. If a pass is made to the neutral player or if the neutral player makes a steal, he can then make a pass to either team. All balls that go out of bounds are brought back into play with a throw-in (U8-U14) or a kick-in (U6).

- *U6:* Players divide into two teams of 2 players each; 20-by-20-yard playing area; 5-minute playing time.
- *U8 and U10:* Players divide into two teams of 3 players each; 25-by-35-yard playing area; 10-minute playing time.
- *U12 and U14:* Players divide into two teams of 4 players each; 35-by-40-yard playing area; 15-minute playing time.

Making Clearances

When the attack plays a ball into the danger zone, the defense has a 50 percent chance of clearing it—meaning that they will send the ball high, wide, and far away from the goal. It is preferable, however, for the defense to intercept or tackle for possession passes, dribbles, or shots, because a counterattack is possible once the defense has gained possession. As defenders become more skillful, many will learn how to turn a clearance into an outlet pass for their team.

Neutral Zone

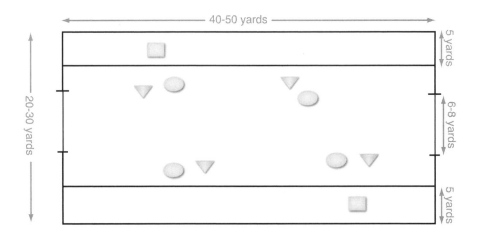

Players divide into two teams and position in a playing area as shown in the diagram with two neutral players stationed in zones on either side of the playing area. The two teams must remain in the center area and only neutral players are allowed in the zones. Players in the center area play a normal soccer match and use defensive clearances with the foot to clear the ball into one of the neutral zones. Neutral players are used to help create good crosses, and a goal may be scored only after a neutral player has crossed the ball.

- *U6:* The activity is not appropriate for this age group.
- *U8 and U10:* Players divide into two teams of 4 players each; 40-by-20-yard playing area; 10-minute playing time.
- *U12 and U14:* Players divide into two teams of 6 players each; 50-by-30-yard playing area; 15-minute playing time.

Goalkeeping

As the last line of defense to prevent a goal, the goalkeeper has the greatest individual defensive responsibility on the team. US Youth Soccer recommends that the position of goalkeeper be introduced in the U10 age group. In the U10 and U12 age groups, the players learning this position will act predominately as shot stoppers in goal. As they learn the techniques and tactics of the position from the U14 age group and up, they will evolve into goalkeepers.

The goalkeeper must be alert and watch the ball at all times. A goalkeeper must be one of the best athletes on the team, given the physical demands of the position. He should be agile and quick, with strong and sure hands, and also must be willing to speak up to organize the team when defending.

The following skills are unique to the position of goalkeeper:

Ready Position

When an opponent has the ball within shooting distance of the goal, the goalkeeper must first assume the ready position. The feet are slightly less than shoulder-width apart, the knees are bent, and the body leans slightly forward. The hands are just above waist level, with palms facing forward and fingers pointing upward. The head is steady and the eyes are focused on the ball (see figure 8.6).

Once an opponent is getting into position to shoot, goalkeepers should maintain their ready position but should come off the goal line toward the ball in an effort to narrow the shooting angle. This maneuver cuts down on the amount of goal that is accessible to the shooter. When the keeper comes off the goal line and moves toward the shooter, the shooter's view of the goal will narrow; therefore, it will be harder for the shooter to get a shot on goal. The tradeoff is that in narrowing the angle to goal, the keeper must be able to react to a shot faster, because the shooter takes it from a closer range.

Coaching Tip

Although the goalkeeper isn't introduced into the game until the U10 age group, players from the U6 to the U14 age groups should be exposed to playing all positions on a soccer team, including the goalkeeper for U10 age groups and up.

Figure 8.6   Ready position for goalkeepers.

Stopping Shots

The technique to shot stopping, or catching the ball, varies depending on the type of shot made. Shots can be on the ground, at waist height, at chest height, or in the air.

Ground Shots   In ground shots, the ball rolls along the ground or just a few inches off of the ground. Use the following points to teach your goalkeepers how to stop a ground shot:

- From the ready position, quickly shuffle sideways to a position between the ball and the goal.
- Bend the legs slightly, with the feet a few inches apart, and bend forward at the waist as the ball arrives (see figure 8.7*a*).
- Extend the arms down, with palms facing forward and hands slightly cupped, and allow the ball to roll up onto the wrists and forearms (see figure 8.7*b*).
- Return to an upright position, clutching the ball tightly to the chest (see figure 8.7*c*).

a   b   c

Figure 8.7 (a-c)   Stopping a ground shot.

Shots at Waist Height   Waist-high shots take a path toward the goalkeeper's waist or slightly above or below it. Use the following points to teach your goalkeepers how to stop a shot at waist height:

- From the ready position, bend forward at the waist as the ball arrives and extend the arms down, palms facing forward and hands slightly cupped (see figure 8.8a).
- Receive the ball on the wrists and forearms, secure it against the chest, and slide the feet backward a few inches to absorb impact (see figure 8.8b).

a   b

Figure 8.8 (a-b)   Stopping a ball at waist height.

Shots at Chest Height   For shots that take a chest-high path, players must use a different grip, called the W-grip (see figure 8.9a), to allow the fingers to cover more surface area of the ball. Younger players with smaller hands can also use the diamond grip (see figure 8.9b), in which they place both the index fingers and thumbs behind the ball to ensure a more secure catch. Goalkeepers of all ages should learn both, since they can be used at all levels.

a   b

Figure 8.9   *(a)* W-grip and *(b)* diamond grip.

Use the following points to teach your goalkeepers how to stop a shot at chest height:

- As the ball arrives, position your hands in the diamond or W-grip position as shown previously in figure 8.9, *a* and *b.*
- Extend your arms, slightly flexed at the elbows, toward the ball and catch the ball with your fingertips (see figure 8.10*a*).
- Withdraw your arms to cushion the impact and secure the ball to your chest (see figure 8.10*b*).

a   b

Figure 8.10 (a-b)   Stopping a ball at chest height or higher.

Lofted Shots   Shots that are at head height or higher are considered lofted shots. They are difficult for young goalkeepers to catch, because doing so requires a greater ability to read the pace, spin, and trajectory of the ball than many young players have developed. Use the following points to teach your goalkeepers how to stop a shot that is lofted high into the air:

- Accurately judge the ball's path and move toward the ball using a one-leg takeoff to generate maximum upward momentum; bend the front leg to increase the height of the jump (see figure 8.11a).
- Extend the arms overhead and attempt to catch the ball at the highest point possible (see figure 8.11b).
- Secure the ball to the chest prior to landing (see figure 8.11c).

a   b   c

Figure 8.11 (a-c)   Stopping a ball that is lofted into the air.

Saving Shots

Saving shots in a basic sense is no different than stopping a shot—both require good catching techniques. For a save, however, the shot does not come directly at the goalkeeper, and he will have to move forward, backward, or laterally to stop the ball. A goalkeeper can save a shot by either diving or collapsing.

Coaching Tip

Teach diving saves to the U12 age group and up. This skill requires good timing, strength, and courage. Learning to dive is for a goalkeeper like learning to fly is for a pilot—the most important part is the landing. Teach players how to land first, then how to take off, and then how to fly across the goal.

Diving   Sometimes your goalkeepers must dive to save a shot. Diving is necessary when an attacker strikes the ball hard and away from the goalkeeper and there is no time to step behind the flight of the ball with the entire body. Instead, the goalkeeper has to extend her body across the goalmouth to get her hands to the ball. Use the following points to teach your goalkeepers how to dive to save shots:

- Step in the direction of the dive with the foot nearest the ball (for example, step with the right foot to dive to the right) and push off that foot to begin the dive (see figure 8.12*a*).

a   b

c   d

Figure 8.12 (a-d)   Diving to save a shot.

- Extend the arms and hands toward the ball and position the hands in a sideways W-grip (see figure 8.12*b*).
- Receive the ball on the fingertips and palms (see figure 8.12*c*).
- Place the lower hand behind the ball, tuck elbows together to the front of the body, and pin the ball to the ground with your upper hand. Contact the ground with your side, not your stomach (see figure 8.12*d*).

Collapsing   Goalkeepers at times (typically for a low-bouncing or ground ball) have to collapse on a ball to secure it in tight quarters. As they secure the ball, they should collapse onto the side of the body, evenly distributing the force of impact and bringing the ball in and the top leg up in a fetal position. Instruct your keepers not to lie on their backs but to stay on their sides so that they are always facing the field of play. This practice is especially important if they have fumbled the ball and need to pounce on it a second time. It also allows goalkeepers to immediately scan the field for where they want to distribute the ball.

Distributing the Ball

After a save, the keeper must distribute the ball to a teammate within six seconds by bowling, throwing, or kicking it. Each method is appropriate for different situations.

Bowling   Bowling the ball is a good choice for distributing the ball when a teammate's distance is 15 yards or less. The motion is similar to that used in regular bowling. Keepers should cup the ball in the palm of the hand, step toward their target with the opposite foot, and release with a bowling-type motion (see figure 8.13). They should release the ball smoothly at ground level so that it doesn't bounce.

> **Coaching Tip**
> The decision about where to distribute the ball is tactical in nature; punting the ball downfield is not necessarily the best choice each time. Teach your players to always distribute to an open teammate, proceeding as for a field player's pass.

Figure 8.13   Distributing the ball by bowling.

Coaching Tip
When bowling or throwing the ball, the goalkeeper's follow-through is crucial to maintaining accuracy. In both cases, teach your goalkeepers that the fingers of the throwing hand should follow through toward the target.

Throwing   To get greater distance when distributing the ball, goalkeepers can throw the ball using an overhand motion similar to throwing a baseball, or they can use a straight-arm overhand or three-quarter motion similar to throwing a javelin. Keepers should hold the ball in the palm of the hand, step toward the target, and use a baseball style (see figure 8.14a) or three-quarter style (see figure 8.14b) throwing motion.

a   b

Figure 8.14   Distributing the ball by throwing (a) baseball style and (b) three-quarter style.

Kicking   Although distributing the ball by using a kick is less accurate than throwing, it can send the ball quickly into the opponent's end of the field. Goalkeepers can use two types of kicks—the full volley punt and the dropkick.

Teach your goalkeepers the following points for the full volley punt:

- Hold the ball in the palm of the hand opposite the kicking foot and extend the arm so that the ball is at waist level (see figure 8.15*a*).
- Step forward with the nonkicking foot, release the ball, and contact the center of the ball with the instep, keeping shoulders and hips square to the target (see figure 8.15*b*).
- Kick through the point of contact, with the kicking foot going waist high.

a   b

Figure 8.15 (a-b)   Distributing the ball using a volley kick.

The dropkick is another kick that goalkeepers can use when distributing the ball. It is similar to the full volley punt, except that the keeper drops the ball (see figure 8.16*a*) and kicks it immediately after it touches the ground (see figure 8.16*b*). The flight of a dropkicked ball is generally lower than that of a full volley punt, making it a better choice on a blustery day.

a   b

Figure 8.16 (a-b)   Distributing the ball using a dropkick.

Punting Contest

Play 1v1 in a field appropriate for the age group. Both players act as goalkeepers and begin the activity in the middle third of the field. One player has the ball to start and punts it toward the other player's goal line. This player tries to catch the ball as soon as possible. From the point on the field where she caught the ball, that player now punts back toward the other player's goal line. The objective is to be the first to force the other player over her goal line.

- *U6 and U8:* The activity is inappropriate for these age groups.
- *U10:* Play on a 60-by-45-yard field.
- *U12:* Play on an 80-by-55-yard field.
- *U14:* Play on a 105-by-65-yard field.

Defensive Set Play Techniques

Defensive techniques, like offensive ones, require players to utilize the basic soccer skills they have learned. However, they must not only know how to perform specific kicking techniques, they must also learn how to successfully defend against these kicks. Practicing defensive set plays teaches them how to defend not only as individual players but also as a team.

Corner Kicks

The most crucial area for goalkeepers to defend consists of the goal area on out to the penalty spot; it is commonly referred to as the danger zone. Instruct your goalkeeper to try to win any ball within the goal area (i.e., about five to six yards in front of the goal line) but not beyond—unless there is a clear path to the ball. Corner kicks can be defended against either by using a zone defense, with the focus on the near post and far post areas, or by marking man-to-man. You can also combine the two, assigning some players to cover the post areas and others to mark individual attackers.

The defending goalkeeper and field players must turn their hips one quarter turn outward toward the field of play. With this body posture they can see the ball and attacking runs, and they can be in a better position to clear the ball upfield. For the goalkeeper, the technique of catching or punching the ball comes into play at corner kicks. For field players, being able to clear the ball is of utmost importance. They will most likely do so with the head, since most corner kicks are delivered in the air.

Free Kicks (Direct and Indirect)

When defending against a free kick, the goalkeeper decides whether a wall needs to be set up and how many players should go into the wall. These decisions are based on the distance between the ball and the goal and the angle of the ball's path to the goal. The closer the ball is to the danger zone, as shown in figure 8.5 on page 94, the more players will be needed in the wall. Generally, forwards and midfielders should go into the wall and fullbacks should be free for zone or man-to-man marking.

Goal Kicks

When defending against a goal kick, it is best for the defenders simply to assume their normal team positions. If the opponent taking the goal kick places the ball on one side of the goal area for the kick, the defending team may want to shift more players to that side of the field to challenge for the ball once it has cleared the penalty area.

Penalty Kick

When defending against a penalty kick, only the goalkeeper is allowed inside the penalty area until the ball is kicked. Once the ball is kicked, defending players may go into the penalty area, so they must be ready to defend. A goal is not a sure thing on a penalty kick, so the defending players should also be ready to enter the penalty area in case the goalkeeper blocks the ball but is unable to hold it, or in case the ball rebounds off the goal. As the defenders enter the penalty area, the skill they are most likely to use is clearing the ball.

Throw-In

When the attacking team has a throw-in in your half of the field, it is a good idea to mark man-to-man within a 30-yard arc of the point from which the ball is being thrown in. This tactic increases the possibility of a turnover in favor of the defending team.

Defensive Tactical Skills

Proper defending is the springboard to the attack. If your team defends skillfully and intelligently, they are more likely to regain possession of the ball. The defensive tactics that you should teach your players are pressure, cover, recovery, and depth.

Pressure

Pressure is necessary to stop the opponent who is in possession of the ball from shooting, dribbling, or passing straight at your goal. The defender nearest the opponent in possession of the ball applies the pressure. To truly apply pressure, the defender must be near enough to the attacker so that the latter is concerned that the defender might actually be able to get the ball. Typically, the defender must be within two strides of the attacker.

The good news is that U6 and U8 players tend to apply pressure naturally, by all clustering around the ball simultaneously. From the U10 age group on up, however, one player at a time should apply the pressure. As mentioned before, this player is simply the defender closest to the ball; the position he plays in the team formation is immaterial. Pressure is applied by proper marking of the attackers, especially the one in possession of the ball.

Cover

While one player pressures the opponent with the ball, other defenders in the immediate vicinity of the ball should provide cover. One to two players should provide cover by positioning themselves behind (goalside of) the teammate pressuring the opponent in possession of the ball. This tactic will slow down the opponent's attack and buy time for the rest of the defending team to recover into good defending positions.

All players on the team must help to defend. The other players on the defending team should get into team positions to cover the rest of the field, in case passes are made by the attacking team. When the ball moves, the players switch roles without switching positions, so defending players may have to pressure and cover depending on where the ball moves.

Recovery

As soon as they lose possession of the ball to the other team, all players on your team become defenders. One player should apply pressure to the ball to slow down the opposing team's attack. This maneuver buys time for teammates to make recovery runs into good defensive goalside positions or into positions that provide cover for the teammate pressuring the ball. Once teammates have made recovery runs to give cover, the defender pressuring the ball can attempt a tackle. To make good recovery runs into defensive positions, your players must have high levels of self-discipline, fitness, and tactical awareness.

Depth

Depth is the tactical concept of getting into a goalside position between the ball and your goal line. Once defending players have made recovery runs to goalside positions, they should provide depth to the defense by getting into positions across the field, behind the teammates applying pressure or giving cover. If one defender is beaten by the attacker with the ball or by a pass or a shot, the other defenders behind still have a chance at the ball. Thus, if the player in possession eludes his defender, the covering defender is on hand to resume the pressure; if the attacker passes, covering defenders are in position to intercept or immediately mark the receiver.

9

Coaching on Game Day

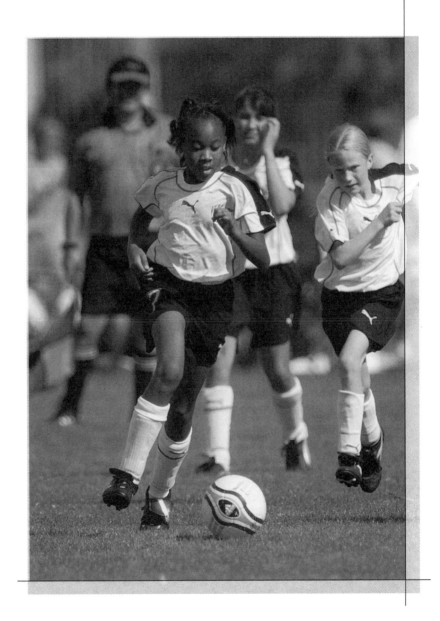

Games provide opportunities for your players to show what they've learned in practice. Just as your players' focus shifts on game days from learning and practicing to competing, your focus shifts from teaching skills to coaching players as they perform those skills in games. Of course, the game is a teaching opportunity as well, but the focus is on performing what has been learned, participating, and having fun.

In previous chapters you learned how to teach your players techniques and tactics; in this chapter you will learn how to coach your players as they execute those techniques and tactics in games. We provide important coaching principles that will guide you before, during, and after a game.

Before the Game

Many coaches focus on how they will coach only during the actual game; instead, preparations should begin well before the first play of the game. A day or two before a game, you should cover several subjects—in addition to techniques and tactics—to prepare your players for the game. Depending on the age group you are working with, create a specific game plan for the opponent based on information that is available to you, make decisions on specific team tactics that you want to use, and discuss pregame particulars such as what to eat before the game, what to wear, and when to be at the field.

Creating a Game Plan

Just as you need a practice plan for what you will cover at each practice, you also need a game plan for game day. As a coach, your game plan for youth soccer will vary depending on the age group you are working with. As you begin planning and mapping out how your game days will progress, keep the following age-related points in mind.

U6 and U8	• Encourage players to try their best. • Relax and let them, and yourself, enjoy the spirit of the game.
U10	• Focus on helping your team execute what they have learned. The strengths and weaknesses of the opposition are of little concern at this age. • Give players simple team formations that make it easy to support each other and execute the techniques and tactics learned in practice. • Remind players to focus on one offensive and one defensive aspect that they have learned for the game. • Give players a starting lineup before kickoff.
U12 and U14	• Help players focus on one or two of the opponent's strengths and weaknesses. • Introduce (as possible) adjustments to play based on the opponent, but continue to give priority to properly executing the techniques and tactics learned in practice. • Introduce more complex team formations that now include a midfield line.

Deciding Team Tactics

Some coaches burn the midnight oil as they devise a complex plan of attack for games. Team tactics at the youth level, however, don't need to be complex—especially for the younger age groups. The main focus should be the importance of teamwork, the responsibility of every player to fulfill their role, and the importance of every player trying their best and working to help teammates. The older the age group and the more familiar you become with your team's tendencies and abilities, the more you can then help them focus on specific tactics.

During the week before a game, coaches of U12 and U14 players should inform them of the tactics that they plan to use against the particular opponent. Regardless of the tactical adjustments you might make for a particular opponent, remember that it is far more important that you teach players the proper execution of individual, group, and team tactics and focus their attention on bringing the skills they have learned in practice to the game.

Coaching Tip
Based on the age level, experience, and knowledge of your players, you may want to let them help you determine the team formation for the game. Allowing player input helps your players learn the game, involves them at a planning level often reserved solely for the coach, and gives them a feeling of ownership. Rather than just carrying out the coach's orders, they're executing the game plan that they helped create.

Discussing Pregame Preparations

Players need to know what to do before a game, such as what and when they should eat on game day, what clothing to wear to the game, what equipment to bring, what time to arrive at the field, and how the warm-up will run. Discuss these particulars with them at the last practice before a game. Here are guidelines for discussing these issues.

Pregame Meal

The general goals of the pregame meal are to fuel the player for the upcoming event, maximize carbohydrate stores, and provide energy to the brain. Some foods, such as those containing carbohydrate and protein, digest more quickly than others; we suggest that players consume these foods rather than fat, which digests more slowly. Good carbohydrate foods include spaghetti, rice, and bran. Good protein foods include low-fat yogurt and boneless, skinless chicken. Players should eat foods that they are familiar with and that they can digest easily. Big meals should be eaten three to four hours before the contest. Players who don't have time for a big meal can consume sport beverages and replacement meals.

Many soccer games are played early in the morning at the youth level, particularly for the U6 and U8 age groups, so a light breakfast an hour or two before the game is best. However, you do not need to awaken a 5-year-old to eat a pregame meal at 6 A.M. for an 8 A.M. kickoff. A light snack before the game is acceptable in these situations.

Clothing and Equipment

Instruct players to wear their team shirts and shorts (or uniforms) and knee-high stockings to the field. They should put on soccer shoes and shin guards once they arrive at the field. You should also teach children to take off their soccer shoes and shin guards immediately after the game. This practice extends the life of the equipment and gives the lower legs and feet a chance to recover through improved circulation.

Youth players from the U6 to U14 age groups should typically wear molded or turf shoes. All cleats, studs, or bars on shoes must be not less than one-half inch wide and not longer than three-fourths of an inch. Aluminum, leather, rubber, nylon, and plastic cleats are legal. Screw-in studs, however, should only be used by adolescent and older players (U15 to U19) and should not be used at the younger levels.

Players may not wear equipment with projecting metal or other hard plates or with exposed sharp edges, such as metal knee braces or hard casts. They also may not wear pads containing hard or unyielding materials, even those covered with soft padding.

Arrival Time

Your players need to adequately warm up before a game, so instruct them to arrive early enough before game time to go through the team warm-up (which you will read about in a later section) and tell them where on the field they should gather. The appropriate amount of time depends on the age group of the team. Following are suggested times for youth age groups.

- *U6 and U8:* 10 minutes before kickoff
- *U10:* 15 minutes before kickoff
- *U12:* 20 minutes before kickoff
- *U14:* 25 minutes before kickoff

Also, consider making a team rule stating that players must show up at a predesignated time before a game and go through the complete team warm-up, or they won't start.

Warm-Up

Players need to prepare both physically and mentally for a game once they arrive at the field, and physical preparation involves warming up. We've suggested that players arrive 10 to 25 minutes before the game to warm up, depending on the age group. Make the game warm-up similar to practice warm-ups. It is also a good idea to walk through the steps for how the team will take the field and where on the field the players will warm up. The warm-up should consist of a few brief games or activities that focus on skill practice, stretches, and range-of-motion exercises. Following are suggested warm-up activities for youth age groups.

- *U6:* Players warm up with the ball individually by practicing skills such as dribbling and juggling.
- *U8:* Players begin with an individual warm-up and then move into pairs and do simple passing and receiving activities.
- *U10-U14:* Players begin with an individual warm-up and then move into group activities such as a small-sided game (5v5); include a warm-up for goalkeepers that focuses on their skills. U14 players may also want to practice their part in set plays.

Refrain from delivering a long-winded pep talk, but you can help players mentally prepare for the game by reminding them of the skills they've been working on in recent practices and focusing their attention on what they've been doing well. Take time also to remind players that they should work as a team, play hard and smart, and have fun.

Unplanned Events

Part of being prepared to coach is to expect the unexpected. What do you do if players are late? What if you have an emergency and can't make the game or will be late? What if the game is rained out or otherwise postponed? Being prepared to handle out-of-the-ordinary circumstances will help you if and when unplanned events happen.

If players are late, you may have to adjust your starting lineup. Although this may not be a major inconvenience, stress to your players that there are important reasons for being on time. First, part of being a member of a team is being committed to and responsible for the other members. When players don't show up or show up late, they break that commitment. Second, players need to warm up to physically and mentally prepare for the game. Skipping the warm-up risks injury.

A time may come when an emergency causes you to be late or miss a game. In these cases, notify your assistant coach (if you have one), your team manager, or the league coordinator. If notified in advance, another volunteer or a parent of a player might be able to step in for the game.

Coaching Tip

Although the site coordinator and officials have formal responsibilities for facilities and equipment, you should know what to look for to ensure that the game is safe for all players (see Facilities and Equipment Checklist in appendix A on page 140). You should arrive at the field 5 to 10 minutes earlier than you asked the players to arrive so that you can check the field, check in with the site coordinator and officials, and greet your players as they arrive to warm up.

Communicating with Parents

The groundwork for your communication with parents will have been laid in the parent orientation meeting, through which parents learned the best ways to support the efforts of their kids (and the whole team) on the field. Help parents judge success based not just on the outcome of the game, but also on how the kids are improving their performances.

If parents yell at the kids for their mistakes during the game, make disparaging remarks about the officials or opponents, or shout instructions for which tactics to use, ask them to stop and to instead support the team through their comments and actions. These standards of conduct should be covered in the preseason parent orientation.

When time permits, as parents gather at the field before a game and before the team takes the field, you can let them know in a general sense what the team has been focusing on during the past week and what your goals are for the game. The parents can be a great asset to the coaches and the team by applauding the efforts of the kids on the field. Their support is especially helpful when the coach has prepped them on what to cheer for in relation to the new techniques and tactics the players are learning. Your players must come first during this time, however, so focus on the kids during the pregame warm-up.

After a game, quickly come together as a staff and decide what to say to the team. Then informally assess with parents, as the opportunity arises, how the team did based not on the outcome, but on meeting performance goals and playing to the best of their ability. Help parents see the contest as a process, not solely as a test that is pass-fail or win-lose. Encourage parents to reinforce that concept at home. For more information on communicating with parents, see page 15 of chapter 2.

Sometimes a game must be postponed because of inclement weather or for reasons such as unsafe field conditions. If the postponement takes place before game day, call every member of your team to let them know. If it happens while the teams are on the field preparing for the game, gather your team members and explain why the game has been postponed. Make sure that all your players have a ride home before you leave—you should be the last to go.

During the Game

Throughout the game, you must keep the competition in proper perspective and help your players do the same. Observe how your players execute techniques and tactics and how well they play together. These observations can help you decide appropriate practice plans for the following week. Let's take a more detailed look at your responsibilities during a game.

Keeping a Proper Perspective

Winning games is the short-term goal of your soccer program. The long-term goals are equally important: learning the techniques, tactics, and rules of soccer; becoming fit; and becoming good sports in soccer and in life. Your young players are winning when they are becoming better human beings through their participation in soccer. You have the privilege of setting the tone for how your team approaches the game. Keep winning and all aspects of the competition in proper perspective, and your young charges will most likely follow suit.

Tactical Decisions

Although you may not be called on to create a complex game strategy, as mentioned earlier, you are called on to make tactical decisions throughout a game. You must make decisions about who starts the game, when to enter substitutes, whether to make slight adjustments to your team's tactics, and how to deal with players' performance errors.

Starting and Substituting Players

When considering playing time, make sure that everyone on the team gets to play at least half of each game. This principle should guide you as you consider starting and substitution patterns. We suggest you consider two options in substituting players:

1. *Substitute individually.*

   Replace one player with another. This method offers you a lot of latitude in deciding who goes in when, and it gives you the most combinations of players throughout the game. Another advantage is that it does not disrupt the rhythm of the team. It can be hard to keep track of each child's playing time, but assigning an assistant or a parent this task can make it easier. Be aware that national rules require a 50 percent playing time for all players.

2. *Substitute after quarters or at halftime.*

   The advantages of substituting players after each quarter are that you can easily track playing time and players know how long they will be in before they might be replaced. Some coaches choose to make substitutions only at halftime.

Adjusting Team Tactics

As mentioned earlier in this chapter, you will make few, if any, tactical adjustments during a game. It is far more important for your players to focus on properly executing the tactics you have taught them during practice than on making adjustments during the game. For the U6, U8, and U10 age groups, do not plan on making any tactical adjustments during the game. For the U12 and U14 age groups, make only minor adjustments that fall within the scope of what the players have already learned. You may want to consider the following questions when adjusting team tactics:

- How does your opponent usually initiate their attacks? Do they aim to get around, over, or through your defense? Identifying their strategy can help you make defensive adjustments.
- Who are the strongest players on the opposing team? The weakest players? As you identify strong players, you'll want to assign your more skilled players to mark them.
- Are the opponent's forwards fast and powerful? Do they come to the ball, or do they try to run behind the defense and receive passes? Their mode of attack should influence how you instruct your players to mark them.
- On defense, does your opponent play a high-pressure game, or do they retreat once you've gained possession of the ball? Each type of defense could call for a different strategy.

Determining the answers to such questions can help you formulate an effective game plan and make proper adjustments as the game progresses. However, don't stress tactics too much during a game. Doing so can take the fun out of the game for the players. If you don't trust your memory, carry a pen and pad to note which team tactics and individual skills need attention at the next practice.

Correcting Players' Errors

In chapter 6 you learned about two types of errors: learning errors and performance errors. Learning errors are those that occur because players don't know how to perform a skill. Performance errors are made not because players don't know how to execute the skill, but because they make mistakes in carrying out what they do know.

Sometimes it's not easy to tell which type of error players are making. Knowing your players' capabilities helps you to determine whether they know the skill and are simply making mistakes in executing it or whether they don't know how to perform it. If they are making learning errors, note the problem and cover it at the next practice. Game time is not the time to teach skills.

If they are making performance errors, however, you can help players correct them during a game. Players who make performance errors often do so because they have a lapse in concentration or motivation (or they are simply demonstrating human error). Competition and contact can also

Coaching Tip

Designate an area on the sideline where players gather after coming off the field. In this area, you can speak to them either individually or as a group and make necessary adjustments.

adversely affect a young player's technique, and a word of encouragement about concentration may help. If you do correct a performance error during a match, do so in a quiet, controlled, and positive tone of voice, either during a break or when the player is on the sideline with you.

For those making performance errors, you must determine whether the error is just an occasional error that anyone can make or whether it is an expected error for a youngster at that stage of development. If the latter is the case, then the player may appreciate your not commenting; she knows it was a mistake and may already know how to correct it. On the other hand, perhaps an encouraging word and a coaching cue ("Remember to follow through on your shots!") are just what the player needs. Knowing the players and judging what to say is an essential part of the art of coaching.

Coach and Player Behavior

Another aspect of coaching on game day is managing behavior—both your players' and your own. Being composed and focused during the game is crucial to good performance on the part of both players and coaches.

Coach Conduct

You greatly influence your players' behavior before, during, and after a game. If you're up, your players are more likely to be up. If you're anxious, they'll take notice and the anxiety can become contagious. If you're negative, they'll respond with worry. If you're positive, they'll play with more enjoyment. If you're constantly yelling instructions or commenting on mistakes, it will be difficult for players to concentrate.

Focus instead on positive competition and on having a good time. Let players get into the flow of the game. A coach who overorganizes everything and dominates a game from the touchline is definitely not making the contest fun. So how should you conduct yourself on the touchline? Here are a few pointers:

- Be calm, in control, and supportive of your players.
- Encourage players often during play, but instruct sparingly. Players should focus on their performance, not on directions shouted from the sidelines.
- If you need to instruct a player, do so when you're both on the touchline, in an unobtrusive manner. Never yell at players for making a mistake. Instead, briefly demonstrate or remind them of the correct technique and then encourage them. Tell them how to correct the problem on the field.

You should also make certain that you have discussed touchline demeanor as a staff and that everyone is in agreement about the way they will conduct themselves—then stick with it. Remember, you're not playing for the World Cup. In this program, soccer competitions are designed to help players develop their skills and character and have fun. So coach at games in a manner that helps your players achieve these goals.

Player Conduct

It is the responsibility of coaches and parents to teach good sporting behavior and to keep players under control, from the U6 age group on up. Do so by setting a good example and disciplining when necessary. Set team rules for good behavior. If players attempt to cheat, fight, argue, badger, yell disparaging remarks, and so forth, it is your responsibility to correct the misbehavior. Initially it may mean removing players immediately from the game, letting them calm down, and then speaking to them quietly. Explain that their behavior is not acceptable for your team and that if they want to play, they must not repeat the action.

Consider team rules in these areas of game conduct:

- Player language
- Player behavior
- Interactions with officials
- Discipline for misbehavior
- Dress code for matches

Player Welfare

All players are not the same. Some attach their self-worth to winning and losing. This idea is fueled by coaches, parents, peers, and society, who place great emphasis on winning. Players become anxious when they're uncertain whether they can meet the expectations of others—especially when meeting a particular expectation is important to them also.

If your players look uptight and anxious during a match, find ways to ease their worries about their performance and to reduce the importance they are attaching to the game. Help players focus on realistic personal goals that are attainable and measurable and that will help them improve their performance while they have fun. Another way to reduce anxiety on game day is to stay away from emotional pregame pep talks. Instead, remind players of the techniques and tactics they will use and encourage them to play hard, do their best, and have fun.

When coaching during games, remember that the most important outcome from playing soccer is each player's increased self-worth. Keep that objective firmly in mind and strive to promote it through every coaching decision.

Opponents and Officials

Respect opponents and officials because without them, there wouldn't be a competition. Opponents provide opportunities for your team to test itself,

Keeping the Game Safe

Chapter 4 is devoted to player safety, but it's worth noting here that safety during games can be affected by how officials call the rules. If officials don't call rules correctly and thus risk injury to your players, you must intervene. Voice your concern in a respectful manner that places the emphasis where it should be: on the players' safety. One of the officials' main responsibilities is to look after everyone's safety, and they should work with coaches to protect the players as much as possible. Don't hesitate to address a safety issue with an official when the need arises.

improve, and excel. Officials help provide a fair and safe experience for players and, as appropriate, help them learn the game.

You and your team should show respect for opponents and officials by being polite and putting forth your best efforts. Don't allow your players to trash-talk or taunt an opponent or an official. Such behavior is disrespectful to the spirit of the competition, and you should immediately remove a player from a match, as discussed previously, if he disobeys your team rules in this area.

Remember, too, that officials at this level are quite often teenagers—in many cases not much older than the players themselves—and the level of officiating should be commensurate with the level of play. In other words, don't expect perfection from officials any more than you do from your own players. They won't make every call, especially at younger levels, because to do so would stop the match every 10 seconds. You may find that officials at younger levels call only the most flagrant penalties, those directly affecting the outcome of the game. As long as they are making calls consistently on both sides and addressing the penalties, most of your officiating concerns will be met.

After the Game

When the game is over, join your team in congratulating the coaches and players of the opposing team, and then be sure to thank the officials. Bring players together to cool down briefly and to replenish fluids. Check on any injuries and inform players how to care for them. Be prepared to speak with the officials about problems that occurred during the game. Then hold a brief meeting (which we discuss later) to ensure your players are on an even keel, whether they won or lost.

Reactions After a Game

Your first concern after a game should be your players' attitudes and mental well-being. You don't want them to be too high after a win or too low after a

Coaching Tip
The total time from the start of the cool-down to the conclusion of the postgame meeting should be approximately 2 minutes for the U6 age group, increasing with older groups to a maximum of 10 minutes for the U14 group.

loss. After the game is when you can most influence them to keep the outcome in perspective and settle their feelings.

When celebrating a victory, make sure your team does so in a way that doesn't show disrespect for the opponents. It's appropriate to be happy about a win, but don't allow your players to taunt the opponents or boast about their victory. If they've lost, your team will naturally be disappointed. But if they've made a winning effort, let them know it. Help them be proud and maintain a positive attitude that will carry over to the next practice and game. Winning and losing are a part of life, not just a part of sport. If players learn to handle both well, they'll have a skill they can apply to whatever they do.

Postgame Team Meeting

After the game, gather your team in a designated area for a short meeting. Before this meeting, decide as a staff what to say and who will say it. Be sure that the staff speaks with one voice after the game.

If your players have performed well, compliment and congratulate them. Whether they've won or lost, tell them specifically what they did with proficiency. Such commendation will reinforce their desire to repeat their good performances. Don't use this time to criticize individual performances or thrash out tactical problems, either. You should help players improve their skills, but do so at the next practice—they won't absorb much tactical information immediately after the game.

Finally, make sure your players have transportation home. Be the last one to leave, to ensure full supervision of your players.

10

Developing Season
and Practice Plans

We hope you've learned a lot from this book: what your responsibilities are as a coach, how to communicate well and provide for safety, how to teach and shape skills, and how to coach on game days. But game days make up only a portion of your season—you and your players will spend more time in practices than in competition. How well you conduct training sessions and prepare your players for competition will greatly affect not only your players' enjoyment and success throughout the season but also your own.

Fun Learning Environment

Regardless of what point you're at in your season, work to create an environment that welcomes learning and promotes teamwork. Following are seven tips to help you and your staff get the most out of your practices:

1. Stick to the practice times agreed on as a staff.
2. Start and end each practice as a team.
3. Keep the practice routine as consistent as possible so that the players can feel comfortable.
4. Be organized in your approach by moving quickly from one activity to another and from one stage of training to another.
5. Tell your players what the practice will include before the practice starts.
6. Allow the players to take water breaks whenever possible.
7. Focus on providing positive feedback.

In addition to trying the activities provided throughout chapters 7 and 8 in this book, you may also want to consider using gamelike activities to add variety and make practices more fun. In appendix C on page 150, you will find 19 gamelike activities. Doing gamelike activities during each practice prepares players for many different situations that arise in games.

Season Plans

Your season plan acts as a snapshot of the entire season. Before the first practice with your players, you must sit down as a staff and develop such a plan. To do so, simply write down each practice and game date on a calendar and then go back and number the practices. These practice numbers are the foundation of your season plan. Now you can work through the plan, moving from practice to practice, and outline what you hope to cover in each practice by noting the purpose of the practice, the main skills you will cover, and the activities you will use.

Following is more detailed information about season plans for each age group: U6, U8, U10, U12, and U14.

U6 Season Plan

The players in this age group will be new to playing soccer. The ball-to-player ratio at this age should be 1:1, so you must plan for individual activities in your practice sessions. For the U6 age group, plan to cover the following concepts and skills during the soccer season:

- *Psychology:* Sharing, fair play, parental involvement, how to play (i.e., getting along with others), and emotional management
- *Fitness:* Balancing, running, jumping, introduction to warming up, and movement education
- *Technical skills:* Dribbling and shooting
- *Tactical skills:* Where the field is and which goal to kick at

Coaching Tip

While developing your season plan, keep in mind that you will want to incorporate the games approach into your practices. The games approach is superior to the traditional approach, since it focuses on replicating the game environment. Using gamelike activities better prepares the players, both physically and mentally, for the demands of the game.

U8 Season Plan

Some of the players in this age group will have been exposed to soccer, but others will be new to the sport. The ball-to-player ratios at this age should be 1:1 and 1:2, so prepare for both individual and paired activities during practice sessions. For the U8 age group, plan to cover these concepts and skills during the soccer season:

- *Psychology:* Working in pairs, fair play, parental involvement, how to play (i.e., getting along with others), and emotional management
- *Fitness:* Agility, eye–foot and eye–hand coordination, introduction to cooling down, and movement education
- *Technical skills:* Ball lifting and juggling, block tackle, receiving ground balls with the inside and sole of the foot, shooting with the inside of the foot, toe pass and shot, throw-in, and introduction to the push pass
- *Tactical skills:* Introduction to all positions and their names, 1v1 attack

U10 Season Plan

Many of these kids will have played soccer, but some may still be novices. The ball-to-player ratio should be 1:3, so you can plan for individual, paired, and small group activities. For the U10 age group, you should cover the following concepts and skills during the soccer season:

- *Psychology:* Working in small groups, focusing for one entire half, sensitivity, how to win and lose gracefully, fair play, parental involvement, how to play (i.e., getting along with others), communication, and emotional management
- *Fitness:* Endurance, range of motion, flexibility, and proper warm-up and cool-down (now mandatory)
- *Technical skills:* Running with the ball, passing, instep drive, receiving ground balls with the instep and outside of the foot, receiving bouncing balls with the instep (cushioning) and with the sole-inside-outside of the foot (wedging), dribbling fakes, and introduction to heading and crossing; for goalkeepers—ready stance, diamond grip, holding the ball after a save, W-grip, catching, shots at the keeper, punting, and introduction to goal kicks and throwing
- *Tactical skills:* 1v1 defending, roles of first attacker and defender, 2v1 attacking, man-to-man defense, and introduction to set plays

U12 Season Plan

Most of the players in this age group will have had exposure to soccer, but some may be newer to the sport. The season plan for this age group builds on the U6 to U10 season plans as players practice and refine fundamental skills. The ball-to-player ratio is 1:5, so you can plan for individual, paired, small group, and larger group activities. For the U12 age group, cover the following concepts and skills during the soccer season:

- *Psychology:* Teamwork, confidence, desire, mental rehearsal, intrinsic motivation, handling distress, how to learn from each match, fair play, parental involvement, how to play (i.e., getting along with others), and emotional management
- *Fitness:* Speed, strength, and aerobic exercise
- *Technical skills:* Feints with the ball, receiving balls (ground, bouncing, and air) with various parts of the body (heel, shins, thigh, abdomen, chest, and head), heading (both standing and jumping) to score goals and clear the ball, chipping to score, passing with the outside of the foot, bending shots, crossing to near post and penalty spot spaces, heel pass, kicking and receiving with the inside of the instep, introduction to half-volley and volley shooting, and introduction to slide tackle; for goalkeepers—footwork, bowling, low dives and forward diving, angle play, near post play, saving penalty kicks, and introduction to parrying and boxing

- *Tactical skills:* 2v1 defending, 2v2 attacking and defending, roles of second attacker and defender, combination passing, verbal and visual communication for all positions, commanding the goalmouth for the goalkeeper, half-time analysis, corner kick plays (defending and attacking), kickoff play, wall pass, identifying potential roles for players (goalkeeper, defender, midfielder, or forward), and introduction to principles of defense

U14 Season Plan

Most of the players in this age group have some experience with soccer, but a few may be newer to the sport. The season plan for this age group builds on the U6 to U12 season plans as players further refine the skills they have learned from past years. The season plan for this age group also introduces several new skills, including heading, diving, and collapsing for goalkeepers. The ball-to-player ratio for this age group is 1:8, so you can plan for individual, paired, and both small and large group activities. For the U14 age group, cover the following concepts and skills during the soccer season:

- *Psychology:* Assertiveness, tension control, self-discipline and team discipline, staying focused for an entire match, fair play, parental involvement, how to play (i.e., getting along with others), mental focusing techniques, and emotional management
- *Fitness:* Power, acceleration, anaerobic exercise, and cardiorespiratory and cardiovascular training
- *Technical skills:* Chipping to pass, bending passes, crossing to far post area and top of the penalty area, half-volley and volley shooting, slide tackles, heading to pass, heading backward, diving headers, kicking and receiving with the outside of the instep, outside-of-foot shot, dummying the ball, shoulder charge; for goalkeepers—far post play, medium and high diving, parrying over the crossbar and around the posts, boxing and catching crosses, half volley (drop kick), kick saves, and long overarm throws
- *Tactical skills:* Individual and group tactics, compactness, commanding the goal area for the goalkeeper, role of third defender, making recovery and tracking runs, throw-ins, penalty kick and free kick plays (defending and attacking), defending the defensive third (both the center and flanks), playing in the attacking third within the center and flanks, postgame analysis, checking runs, takeovers, switching positions during the flow of play, providing offensive support out to the penalty spot for the goalkeeper, zone defense, and introduction to the principles of attack

Practice Plans

Coaches rarely believe they have enough time to practice everything they want to cover. Practice plans help you organize your thoughts so that you stay on track with your practice objectives. They also help you better visualize and prepare so that you can run your practices effectively.

First, your practice plans should be age appropriate to the group you are coaching, incorporating all of the skills and concepts you wrote into the season plan for that age group. The core of your practice plan should include activities that move from simple to more complex and that focus on the skills highlighted in the season plan. The plan for each practice should note the practice objective and the equipment necessary to execute specific activities. It should also include a warm-up and a cool-down.

Remember that during the cool-down, coaches should attend to any injuries incurred during practice and make sure that players drink plenty of water. It is also a good idea to have them loosen shoelaces to help circulation in the feet and, beginning with the U10 age group, loosen or take off their shin guards to aid blood flow to the lower legs. Such provisions for player well-being should be part of every practice.

Also know that constructing practice plans requires both organization and flexibility on your part. Don't be intimidated by the amount of material you've listed in your season plan as skills and tactics you want to cover. Pick out a few basics and build your initial practice plans around them; this process will get easier after you've drafted a few plans. Then you can move from teaching simple concepts and skills to drawing up plans that introduce more complex ones. Build in some flexibility; if you find that what you've planned for practice isn't working, have a backup activity that approaches the skill or concept from a different angle. The priorities are to keep your team playing the game and to help everyone have fun while they're learning.

Sample U6 Practice Plan

Objective
Dribbling

Equipment
A ball for each player, 2 small goals (cones or bicycle flags can be used in lieu of goals), 12 cones, 10 training bibs (5 of one color and 5 of another)

Activity	Description	Coaching points
Warm-up (3 min)	Practice balance activities such as standing on one foot, one- and two-leg hopping, and skipping.	• Balance • Agility • Coordination
Ball master (10 min)	Each player has a ball, dribbles to the coach, and hands her the ball. Coach tosses the ball away, and players retrieve the ball and dribble it back to her. Coach can designate a different dribbling challenge to players with each toss.	• Listening skills • Problem solving • Dynamic dribbling
Shadow dribble (5 min)	Each player dribbles a ball and follows the coach, who is also dribbling a ball. Coach executes basic dribbling moves and silly movements for players to mimic. Include dribbling basics and tumbling, balancing, and rhythmic exercises.	• Dribbling and movement enhancement • Decision making
Knee tag (5 min)	Players position with a ball in a 10 × 15 yd area. Players dribble their balls and try to tag others on the knee. Each player gets one point for a tag.	• Physical fitness components • Dribbling and shielding skills • Looking around (vision)
3v3 match (15 min)	Play a 3v3 match according to US Youth Soccer modified rules for the U6 age group. Use two goals, one ball, and no goalkeepers.	• Summation of all challenges for the players (remember—stay out of their way and let them play)
Cool-down (5 min)	Body shapes: Players create as many different shapes as they can with their bodies. Coach prompts change of movement.	• Lowering heart rate and body temperature • Body control • Creativity and fun

Sample U8 Practice Plan

Objective
Ball control

Equipment
A ball for each player, 2 small goals (cones or bicycle flags can be used in lieu of goals), 24 cones, 12 training bibs (6 of one color and 6 of another)

Activity	Description	Coaching points
Warm-up (5 min)	Soccer marbles: Players divide into pairs; each player has a ball on the ground. Player A passes his ball and tries to hit Player B's ball. After both balls stop rolling, Player B makes a pass to try and hit Player A's ball, and so on. Each ball must be stationary before a pass is made. Players may not block the path of the pass.	• Gradual warm-up of the muscles without overexertion • Repeated practice of passing accuracy • Competition and fun
Math dribble (5 min)	Players position, each with a ball, in a 15 × 20 yd area. Coach calls out a number or a simple math addition problem. If coach calls "1 + 1," players quickly form groups of 2. If coach calls out "3," players form groups of 3.	• Keeping the head up • Keeping the ball close using the inside, outside, and soles of feet • Keeping the ball within playing distance (1-3 steps) • Exploding into the space after ball is stopped or direction is changed
Multigate dribbling (10 min)	Players position with a ball in a 25 × 30 yd area with small goals (gates), set up using cones (1-2 steps apart), all around the area at different angles. Coach times the play, and players must count the number of gates that they dribble through in 30 sec (make it exciting for players by counting down the last 10 sec). Players attempt to increase number on future attempts.	• Keeping the ball close using the inside, outside, and soles of feet • Controlled dribbling • Looking around (vision) • Changing pace (exploding through a gate) • Changing direction • Decision making (when another player is occupying a gate, looking for another open gate)

Activity	Description	Coaching points
Multigate passing (10 min)	Players position in pairs with one ball per group in a 25 × 30 yd area with small goals (gates), set up using cones (1-2 steps apart), all around the area at different angles. Pairs move about and pass the ball to their partners through the gates. Play each round for 1 min with the coach keeping time. Take about 30 sec between each round to ask the players how many gates they got through and encourage them to beat their records on the next round. Pairs attempt to increase number on future attempts.	• Keeping the ball close using the inside, outside, and soles of feet • Controlled passing • Looking around (vision) • Change of pace • Change of direction • Decision making
Combat (10 min)	Players divide into two teams (no more than 5 players per team) and position in an open area with no boundaries. Each team lines up single file on opposite sides of the coach, facing the open area. The coach kicks a ball into the open area and the first player from each line chases after the ball. The first player to reach the ball attempts to possess it while the other player tries to steal it. The first player to successfully pass the ball back to the coach's feet gets one point, and the players go to the end of their lines. When the ball is returned to the coach's feet it is immediately kicked into the area again, and the next two players in line chase it. For safety reasons, the coach positions away from the lines once the game begins.	• Quickness and speed • Dribbling for possession (shielding) • Vision (finding the target) • Passing
4v4 match (15 min)	Players divide into teams of 4 and position in standard field for the U8 age group, with no goalkeepers. Balls are scattered around the outside of the field, and teams play 4v4 without the coach serving the balls. When a ball goes out of bounds, a player gets any ball closest to where it went out and puts it into play.	• Playing and having fun • Giving generous praise for effort and hard work
Cool-down (5 min)	The long and the short of it: Players sit on the ground and coach asks them to show how small they can make their bodies, how long, how wide, what shape, and so forth.	• Lowering heart rate and body temperature • Body control • Creativity, imagination, and fun

Sample U10 Practice Plan

Objective
Distribution

Equipment
A ball for each player, 2 regulation goals for the U10 age group (cones or bicycle flags can be used in lieu of goals), 24 cones, 4 corner flags, 22 training bibs (11 of one color and 11 of another)

Activity	Description	Coaching points
Warm-up (10 min)	Players jog in different directions with change of speed; throw the ball up, touch toes (once, twice, etc.), catch; throw the ball up, forward roll, catch; drop the ball to thigh height from chest, catch it at thighs, and quickly bring it to chest (repeat 12 times).	• Increasing circulation and loosening joints • Improving core body strength • Eye–hand coordination, agility, and balance • Improving reflexes
Hit the teammate (10 min)	Players rehearse throwing (bowl and over-arm), goal kick, and punt techniques with a partner. Players position 10 yds apart to start and increase (15-20 yd for U10, 20-25 yd for U12, and 25-30 yd for U14). Players coach each other on proper execution. Coach should also observe body mechanics and provide guidance when necessary.	• Cooperation • Self-challenge • Accuracy of distribution, not distance
From the flanks to the middle (15 min)	Goalkeeper positions in the goal, and 5 players position in the defensive third of the field; 2 players position on each post to challenge the keeper with attempts to score, and 2 wingers position on the touch lines to send in crosses. The keeper saves the cross or shot and distributes to the wingers or to the center midfielder, who then passes out to the wings. Repeat.	• Accuracy of distribution • Ball control
Match condition (15 min)	Players position on a field 60 × 40 yd with two standard goals for the U10 age group. A keeper positions in each goal, with a striker in front of each goal, 2 wings attacking both ways, a center midfielder attacking both ways, and 2 defenders in front of each goal. Goalkeeper starts play with a distribution to a winger, defender, center midfielder, or striker. An attack is made on the opposite goal, and then a counterattack. Goalkeepers should concentrate on accurate distribution and on communication with the player to whom the ball is distributed. Repeat.	• Decision making on where to distribute • Assessing tactical information that the goalkeeper gives during the distribution (man on, turn, etc.)

Activity	Description	Coaching points
6v6 match (25 min)	Play a match according to US Youth Soccer U10 modified rules.	• Observing distribution techniques of the goal keepers
Cool-down (10 min)	Bowling for dollars: All players position in the penalty area with a ball. While holding the ball, players use a bowling motion to roll the ball and try to hit other players in the feet. Stop and do stationary stretching every 30 sec.	• Lowering heart rate and body temperature • Repetition • Accuracy • Timing

Sample U12 Practice Plan

Objective
Spatial awareness

Equipment
A ball for each player, 2 regulation goals for the U12 age group (cones or bicycle flags can be used in lieu of goals), 24 cones, 4 corner flags, 14 training bibs (7 of one color and 7 of another)

Activity	Description	Coaching points
Warm-up (10 min)	Paint the grass: Players position in pairs with 1 ball per group in a 10 × 15 yd area. Players imagine the ball is a paint brush and paint (via passes) as much of the grass in the area as they can. Play three 30-sec rounds with a stretch between each.	• Increasing circulation and loosening joints • Passing and receiving techniques • Communication and problem solving
Sequence passing (15 min)	Players divided into groups of 5 (up to 7 players if necessary), with two or three groups using the same field. Coach numbers each player (1 through 5), and players must pass to each other in that sequence (i.e., 1 to 2, 2 to 3, and so on) with the last player (5) passing back to the first player (1). Players must pass on the move—no standing allowed. Each group must play through, over, and around the other groups, which increases the demand on vision, communication, and off-the-ball movement. Variations include reducing the playing area to half the original size or having each group start with one ball and adding a second ball as players improve.	• Vision and communication between players without the pressure of opponents • Passing and receiving techniques • Improving rhythm of play and timing of support runs • Getting into the field of vision of the teammate with the ball • Dynamic runs
Crossing game (15 min)	Players divide into groups of 4 in a 40 × 30 yd playing area. Use corner flags or tall cones as goals; set them up diagonally from one another, 10 yd in from the goal line. Play a normal 4v4 match except players can score from either side of the goal, and the game doesn't stop after a goal is scored. Because of the angled goals there will be more crosses into areas in front of the goalmouth. Many goals can be scored under match conditions in a short time period. Teamwork in preparing attack and defense will improve.	• Group movement (tactics) • Transition • Dribbling, passing, receiving, shooting, heading, tackling, and crossing techniques • Improving fitness in a fun and competitive fashion

Activity	Description	Coaching points
Three-team game (20 min)	Players divide into three groups of 5 and position on a standard field for the U12 age group. A goalkeeper positions in each goal and acts as his own team. Divide field into thirds (defensive, midfield, and attacking), with each group (X, Z, and O) positioned in a third. The group in the midfield third (Z) has the ball and chooses a goal to attack. They then play against the group positioned in the third that they chose (X). The group at the other end (O) rests. Only the group in possession of the ball may enter the midfield third. If the midfield group (Z) scores, they keep the ball, go back to the midfield third, and attack the resting group's (O's) goal. If the defending group (X) wins the ball and is able to move it into the midfield third, the original midfield group (Z) stays in the third at X's original end, and the original defending group (X) attacks against the original resting group (O). Each group keeps track of its own score.	• Complex game environment • High level of concentration • Creating space
All up and all back (20 min)	Play a full field 8v8 match and follow the US Youth Soccer rules for the U12 age group. A line of small disc cones marks the halfway line, and a goal only counts when all field players of the attacking team are over the halfway line. If any of the field players are not over the halfway line and in the opponent's half of the field, the goal does not count and a goal kick follows. Once players are ready, the coach can introduce another challenge and require that all defending players must be in their half of the field or the goal counts double.	• Team communication • Improving off-the-ball runs • Vision • Improving fitness • Compactness
Cool-down (10 min)	High five: All players position in center circle and move about. As players approach each other, they jump as high as they can and high-five one another (with both hands) above their heads. Players should try to high-five every teammate. Stop and do stationary stretching every 30 sec.	• Lowering heart rate and body temperature • Fun

Sample U14 Practice Plan

Objective
Penetrating passes

Equipment
A ball for each player, 2 regulation goals for the U14 age group (cones or bicycle flags can be used in lieu of goals), 24 cones, 4 corner flags, 16 training bibs (8 of one color and 8 of another)

Activity	Description	Coaching points
Warm-up (10 min)	Working in pairs, players pass back and forth using a variety of passing techniques. Begin with unlimited touches and work up to one-touch passing.	• Focus • Increasing blood flow and breathing rate • Repetition of passing techniques
5v2 match (10 min)	In a circle (5 yd radius) or rectangle (20 × 15 yd) playing area, 5 offensive players and 2 defensive players play a game of keep-away. The offensive players work to keep possession from the defensive players and look for opportunities to split them with a pass. Coach should encourage offensive players to try various types of passes, both on the ground and in the air.	• Opening hips on passes • Vision for attacking players (being aware of where the defending players are) • Creating passing lanes • Teammate support
Short-short-long (10 min)	Form groups of 7 players, with all groups playing in one-half of the field. Players are on the move at all times and execute passing combinations of two short passes followed by a long pass (on the ground or in the air) to the teammate in the group farthest from the first attacker. Two players off the ball must move to support the receiver, who must play a first-touch knockoff to the supporting players. Resume sequence.	• Improving passing and receiving techniques • Moving off the ball at proper angles • Vision
End-zone game (15 min)	Play 4v4 (up to 7v7 if necessary) in a 30 × 25 yd (up to 60 × 45 yd) playing area with an end zone (3 yd into the area) marked at each end. Players must make a pass to a teammate running into the end zone, with the pass collected under good control, to be awarded one point. When a team scores, they then turn and attack the opposite end zone.	• Width, depth, and support in the team shape • Movement of players off the ball • Decision making on when to dribble or make a pass • Ability of front player to receive and protect the ball under pressure

Activity	Description	Coaching points
Half-field match (15 min)	Play a half-field 6v4 match with one goal-keeper in front of the goal and follow the US Youth Soccer rules for the U14 age group. Players must pay special attention to opportunities for penetrating in the flank zones.	• Combination passing • Recognizing possession and penetration opportunities
8v8 match (20 min)	Play a full-field 8v8 match with two goal-keepers and follow the US Youth Soccer rules for the U14 age group.	• Decision making • Recognizing the tactical situation of when to penetrate. • Technique of penetration
Cool-down (10 min)	Inside the penalty area, players slowly jog from one side to the other and then do two stationary stretches. Reduce space to that between the penalty spot and one side of the penalty area, and again players slowly jog from side to side and do two different stationary stretches. Then players move into the goal area, slowly jog from side to side, and do two different stationary stretches.	• Lowering heart rate and body temperature • Promoting team unity

Appendix A

Related Checklists and Forms

This appendix contains checklists and forms that will be useful in your soccer program. All checklists and forms mentioned in the text can be found here. You may reproduce and use these checklists and forms as needed for your soccer program.

Facilities and Equipment Checklist

Field Surface

- ❏ Sprinkler heads and openings are at grass level.
- ❏ The field is free of toxic substances (lime, fertilizer, and so on).
- ❏ The field is free of low spots or ruts.
- ❏ The playing surface is free of debris.
- ❏ No rocks or cement slabs are on the field.
- ❏ The field is free of protruding pipes, wires, and lines.
- ❏ The field is not too wet.
- ❏ The field is not too dry.
- ❏ The field lines are well marked.

Outside Playing Area

- ❏ The edge of the playing field is at least six feet from trees, walls, fences, and cars.
- ❏ Nearby buildings are protected (by fences, walls) from possible damage during play.
- ❏ Storage sheds and facilities are locked.
- ❏ The field area (ground surface and equipment) is in safe condition.
- ❏ The fences or walls lining the area are in good repair.
- ❏ Sidewalks are without cracks, separations, or raised concrete.

Equipment

- ❏ Goals are held securely together.
- ❏ Goals are secured to the ground.
- ❏ Players' equipment passes inspection, fits properly, and complies with the rules.

From *Coaching Youth Soccer,* 4th ed., by ASEP, 2006, Champaign, IL: Human Kinetics.

Informed Consent Form

I hereby give my permission for _____ to participate in
_____during the athletic season beginning on _____.
Further, I authorize the school or club to provide emergency treatment of any injury or illness my child may experience if qualified medical personnel consider treatment necessary and perform the treatment. This authorization is granted only if I cannot be reached after reasonable effort to do so.

Parent or guardian: _____

Address: _____ Phone: (   )_____

Cell phone: (   )_____ Beeper number: (   )_____-__

Other person to contact in case of emergency:_____

Relationship to person:_____ Phone: (   )_____

Family physician: _____ Phone: (   )_____

Medical conditions (e.g., allergies, chronic illness): _____

_____

_____

_____

My child and I are aware that participating in _____ is a potentially hazardous activity. We assume all risks associated with participation in this sport, including but not limited to falls, contact with other participants, the effects of weather and traffic, and other reasonable conditions of risk associated with the sport. All such risks to my child are known and appreciated by my child and me.

We understand this informed consent form and agree to its conditions.

Child's signature: _____ Date: _____

Parent's or guardian's signature:_____ Date:_____

From *Coaching Youth Soccer,* 4th ed., by ASEP, 2006, Champaign, IL: Human Kinetics. Reprinted, by permission, from M. Flegel, 2004, *Sport first aid*, 3rd ed. (Champaign, IL: Human Kinetics), 15.

Injury Report Form

Date: _____ Time: _____ A.M. / P.M.

Location: _____

Player's name: _____

Age: _____ Date of birth: _____

Type of injury: _____

Anatomical area involved: _____

Cause of injury: _____

_____

_____

Extent of injury: _____

_____

_____

Person administering first aid (name): _____

First aid administered: _____

_____

Other treatment administered: _____

_____

Referral action: _____

_____

_____

_____

Signature of person administering first aid: _____

Date: _____

From *Coaching Youth Soccer,* 4th ed., by ASEP, 2006, Champaign, IL: Human Kinetics.

Emergency Information Card

Player's name:_____ Sport:_____

Age:_____ S.S. #:_____

Address:_____

Phone:_____

Provide information for parent or guardian and one additional contact in case of emergency:

Parent's or guardian's name:_____

Address:_____

Phone:_____ Other phone:_____

Additional contact's name:_____

Relationship to player:_____

Address:_____

Phone:_____ Other phone:_____

Insurance Information

Name of insurance company:_____

Policy name and number:_____

Medical Information

Physician's name:_____ Phone:_____

Is your child allergic to any drugs?   YES   NO

If so, what?_____

Does your child have other allergies (e.g., bee stings, dust)?_____

_____

Does your child have any of the following? *asthma diabetes epilepsy*

Is your child currently taking medication?   YES   NO

If so, what? _____

Does your child wear contact lenses?   YES   NO

Is there additional information we should know about your child's health or physical condition?   YES   NO

If yes, please explain: _____

_____

Parent's or guardian's signature: _____ Date:_____

From *Coaching Youth Soccer,* 4th ed., by ASEP, 2006, Champaign, IL: Human Kinetics.

Emergency Response Card

Be prepared to give the following information to an EMS dispatcher. Note: Do not hang up first. Let the EMS dispatcher hang up first.

Caller's name: _____

Telephone number from which the call is being made: _____

Reason for call: _____

_____

How many people are injured: _____

Condition of victim(s): _____

_____

First aid being given:_____

_____

Location: _____

Address: _____

City: _____

Directions (e.g., cross streets, landmarks, entrance access, etc.):

From *Coaching Youth Soccer,* 4th ed., by ASEP, 2006, Champaign, IL: Human Kinetics.

Appendix B

Soccer Terms

assistant referee—An official who supports the head referee. Assistant referees watch the touchlines and use flags to signal the referee when various situations occur, such as a foul the referee might have missed, an offside, or an out-of-bounds ball.

ballside—The side of the field on which the ball is in play at a given time.

beat—To dodge a tackle by faking a maneuver.

block tackle—An attempt to prevent an attacker from maintaining possession of the ball by blocking the ball with the inside of the foot while the attacker is attempting to dribble it the other way.

caution—A disciplinary action against player misconduct, initiated by the referee and signaled with a yellow card. It is officially recorded, and a second offense can cause the player to be ejected from the game (signaled by a red card).

center circle—The circle in the center of the field surrounding the kickoff spot, outside of which the defending team must remain until the ball is put into play at a kickoff.

center forward—The centermost forward, who usually leads the forwards' attack and scores most of the goals.

center mark—The spot in the center circle (also the midpoint of the halfway line) where the ball is positioned for kickoffs.

charging—Using the shoulder to bump the shoulder of an attacker in order to take away the ball (the only deliberate body contact that is legal in soccer).

corner arc—The four one-yard arcs, one in each corner of the field of play, from which players take corner kicks.

corner flags—The flags that mark the corners of the playing field, which must remain in place during corner kicks.

corner kick—A direct free kick taken from a corner arc by a member of the attacking team if the ball goes out of bounds across the goal line and was last touched by a member of the defending team.

cover—A defensive concept in which a defender goes goalside to provide backup for a teammate who is challenging an attacker for possession of the ball.

defenders—Defenders play near their own team's goal and try to prevent the other team from shooting the ball. They also receive the ball from the goalkeeper and move the ball up the field to begin the offense.

direct free kick—A free kick that may go directly into the goal to score, without another player having to touch the ball. Also refers to bad conduct or a foul resulting in a penalty that awards a direct free kick to the opponent.

diving—A move by which the goalkeeper stops or repels balls (usually low or medium-high) aimed at the goal.

dribbling—Controlling and moving the ball along the ground with light touches of the feet.

drop ball—A ball the referee drops between two opposing players to resume the game after play has been stopped (but no penalty has been called); a player may score a goal directly from a drop-ball kick. The ball is dropped at the spot where it was last in play, unless it was in the goal area. In the latter case the referee drops the ball at the nearest point outside the goal area.

ejection—Banishing a player from the field. It is a disciplinary action (signaled by a red card and put into the official record) that the referee takes against a player who has committed a personal foul or a deliberate hand ball.

far post—The goalpost farthest from the ball at a given time.

feinting—Using a fake move to fool an opponent.

first-touch pass—Kicking or heading the ball to pass it, without first stopping it.

forwards—Forwards play closer to the other team's goal and shoot the ball more than other players. The forwards that play nearest the touchlines are called wings; those in the middle of the field are referred to as strikers.

free kick—A placekick awarded to a team when a player on the other team receives a penalty. It can be a direct kick or an indirect kick, depending on the seriousness of the opposing team's offense. Players on the offending team must stay a certain number of yards (related to the size of the center circle) away from the ball until the kicker moves it, unless they are between the goalposts of their own goal line.

fullback—A player who is part of a team's back line of defense, just in front of the goalkeeper. The primary assignment of fullbacks (also called backs) is to repel attacks on their team's goal.

give-and-go—A pass in which a receiver is used to redirect the path of the ball while the passer runs to get open to receive a return pass. It is also called a wall pass.

goal—The area into which players try to shoot the ball to score points. A goal sits in the middle of the goal line at each end of the playing field but extends past the field itself. It is marked by two goalposts, a crossbar, and netting.

goal area—The small box immediately in front of the goal, from which players take the goal kick.

goal kick—A placekick that a defending player takes from the goal area when a ball that an attacking player was the last to touch goes out of bounds across the goal line. All members of the attacking team must stay outside the penalty area until the ball clears it and is back in play.

goal line—The end line of the field, on which the goal sits. The goal line runs from corner to corner.

goal side—Any position between the ball and the goal of the defending team.

goalkeeper—A goalkeeper plays in front of the goal and tries to prevent the ball from getting into the goal. The goalkeeper is the only player allowed to use the hands to block shots and to initiate the offense from within the team's penalty area.

halfway line—The line that runs across the field of play from touchline to touchline and divides the field in half.

handball—Intentional use of the hands on the ball by any player except the goalkeeper.

heading—Propelling and guiding the ball by striking it with the forehead, between the eyebrows and the hairline.

holding—Using the hands or arms to obstruct the movements of an opposing player, constituting a personal foul.

indirect free kick—A free kick that must be touched by a player other than the one who kicked it before it can score a goal; also refers to a particular penalty the referee calls for minor fouls.

juggling—A training technique used to develop ball control, in which a player uses any part of the body other than the hands and arms to keep the ball in the air continuously.

kickoff—A placekick that starts the game, restarts the game after a goal is scored, or starts the second half of the game. It is taken from the center spot, and players may score a goal directly from a kickoff; however, players must remain outside the center circle until the ball is in play.

man-to-man defense—A defensive strategy in which each defending player is responsible for marking a specific offensive player.

marking—Defending against an opponent.

midfielders—Midfielders are all-purpose players who take shots and try to steal the ball from the other team. They are transition players, helping move the ball from defense to offense. Their position is named appropriately, since they play between forwards and defenders on the field.

near post—The goalpost nearest the ball at a given time.

obstruction—Player action that deliberately hinders an opponent's progress instead of playing the ball.

off the ball—Describes players who are not near the ball.

offside—Getting between the other team's goal line and the ball at the moment the ball is played by a teammate. The offside rule has exceptions: A player cannot be called offside if an opponent, not a teammate, last played the ball; if she received the ball directly from a corner kick, goal kick, throw-in, or drop ball; if she doesn't go closer to the opponent's goal line than at least two opponents are; or if she is in her own team's half of the field.

out of play—Description for a ball that has gone completely across the goal line or a touchline.

passing—Kicking or heading a ball to direct it toward a teammate.

penalty arc—An arc drawn outside the penalty area, at a radius similar to the one for the center circle, from the penalty spot. No players are allowed within this arc when a penalty kick is being taken.

penalty area— The large box in front of the goal, within which the goalkeeper may legally use hands on the ball. When the defending team commits, inside the penalty area, a foul that normally gives the offense a direct free kick, the foul instead results in a penalty kick.

penalty kick—A direct free kick that a referee awards to the offensive team when a member of the defensive team commits a major foul while inside his own team's penalty area. The attacker takes the kick from the penalty spot and can score a goal directly from the kick. The goalkeeper must stay on his team's goal line until the ball is kicked, but all other players must stay outside the penalty area, no closer than 10 yards from the penalty spot, until the attacker kicks the ball.

penalty mark—A location 12 yards in front of the midpoint of the goal line. Other names for it are the penalty spot or penalty kick spot; it is the place from which players take penalty kicks.

placekick—A kick taken from a stationary position that starts or restarts the game.

punching—Hitting the ball with the fists to deflect the ball or save a goal. Only the goalkeeper may punch the ball, and only from within the penalty area.

punt—A kicking technique in which the goalkeeper drops the ball and then kicks it before it hits the ground.

receiving—The act of first collecting the ball and then getting control of it before putting it into play.

referee—The official who has overall responsibility for a match and works with two assistant referees.

restart—Any of the methods for starting up play again after it has been stopped—the placekick, the throw-in, and the drop ball.

save—The goalkeeper's successful attempt to prevent a score by catching or repelling a ball headed for the goal.

shielding—Positioning oneself between the ball and an opponent while dribbling in order to keep the opponent from gaining possession of the ball.

shooting—Attempting to score by kicking the ball toward the goal.

tackling—Using the feet or charging with the shoulder to gain possession of the ball from an opponent.

throw-in—A way to get the ball back into play after it has gone out of bounds over a touchline. Standing at the point at which the ball left the field, the player (one of the opponents of the player who last touched the ball) holds the ball over her head with both hands and throws it onto the field. She must keep part of each foot on the ground, either behind or on the touchline. Players can score a goal directly from a throw-in.

touchline—The sideline that runs the length of the field of play from corner to corner.

trapping—Stopping the ball while in a stationary position.

volley kick—A kick that a player takes when the ball is still in the air.

wall—A way to help the goalkeeper defend against free kicks. At least two other defensive players line up with the keeper to form a human barrier between the kicker and the goal, but they must stand a required distance away from the ball (equal to the radius of the center circle for that age group).

weak side—The side of the field where the ball is not in play at a given time.

wingbacks—Fullbacks assigned to positions near the touchlines (also known as outside backs), who with the other defenders and goalkeeper form the line of defense closest to their own goal.

wingers—Forwards assigned to positions near the touchlines (also called outside forwards), whose responsibility is to bring the ball up the sidelines and pass into scoring range for other attacking players.

wings—The sides of the field, along the right and left touchlines.

zone defense—A defensive strategy in which defenders cover a specific area of the field rather than a specific defender; they must cover any opponent who enters their zone.

Appendix C

19 Gamelike Activities

The 19 gamelike activities found here are for use in your soccer program. These activities differ from those found in chapters 7 and 8, because they focus on creating gamelike scenarios, distinguishing between offensive and defensive teams, and setting up scoring situations. As a youth soccer coach, you will want to use gamelike activities during practices to keep motivation high and make the sport fun.

Dribble Attack

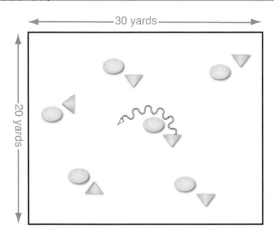

Goal

To develop and encourage dribbling with both feet

Description

Play 3v3 in an area 30 yards long by 20 yards wide, as shown in the diagram. Offensive and defensive players (3 of each) pair up and position anywhere inside the playing area (a second playing area can be set up if there are more than 6 players). Attacking players must dribble past the defending players. The defending players should try to gain possession of the ball and then (if they do) dribble past an opponent. Players may dribble in any direction inside the playing area to start, and play can progress to a variation in which the coach gives the attack a direction (e.g., dribbling to a specified goal line). The offense earns 1 point whenever a player is able to dribble past a defender. The offense is allowed to pass past a defender in an effort to advance the ball but receives no points for doing so.

- *U6:* Play two 2-minute rounds; focus only on attackers properly dribbling past defenders.
- *U8:* Play two 2-minute rounds.
- *U10:* Play three 3-minute rounds.
- *U12:* Play four 4-minute rounds.
- *U14:* Play five 5-minute rounds.

Variations

- To make the game easier for younger or less skilled players, play 3v2 or 2v1.
- To make the game more challenging for older or more skilled players, award an additional point for offensive players who dribble past a defender while using their weak foot or award points only for dribbling past a defender with the weak foot.

Four-Goal Mayhem

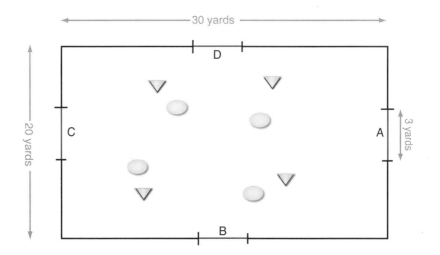

Goal

To encourage players to turn and change direction

Description

Play 4v4 in a 30-by-20-yard playing area as shown in the diagram, with 3-yard-wide goals set up at the center of each of the four sidelines. Each team consists of 4 players, with no goalkeepers. To start, players position in the center of the area and the coach drops the ball in the middle. One team attacks goals A and B and defends goals C and D; the other attacks goals C and D and defends goals A and B. Teams are awarded 1 point for each pass, dribble, or shot through the goals. Each time a point is scored, the coach restarts the game by dropping the ball in the middle, as when the game began. When the ball goes out of play, the game is restarted with a throw-in.

- *U6:* The activity is inappropriate for this age group.
- *U8 and U10:* Play for 5 minutes or until 5 points are scored.
- *U12 and U14:* Play for 10 minutes or until 10 points are scored.

Variations

- To make the game easier for younger or less skilled players, allow both teams to score on any goal.
- To make the game more challenging for older or more skilled players, reduce the space to 20 by 20 yards (creating more pressure to turn in tight spaces), play 2v2 in a 20-by-15-yard area with four goalkeepers, or increase the area to 50 by 40 yards and play 6v6.

Short and Sharp

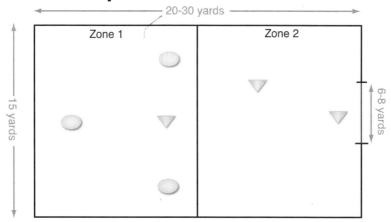

Goal

To develop short passing technique

Description

Play 3v3 in a playing area as shown in the diagram, with one goal set up at the far end. Offensive and defensive teams consist of 3 players each. Divide the area's length into two zones. The 3 offensive players and 1 defensive player position in zone 1, and the remaining defensive players position in zone 2, one of them acting as a goalkeeper.

Play begins with a kick-in from the goal line, and players play 3v1 in zone 1. The offensive team must pass three times before moving into zone 2, where they will again play 3v1 and make three passes before shooting on goal. Defenders must stay in their zones. Offense receives 2 points for successfully passing in zone 1, 2 points for successfully passing (maintaining possession of the ball) in zone 2, and 1 point for a goal. If a defender wins the ball, the game restarts with a free pass between attackers.

- *U6:* The activity is inappropriate for this age group.
- *U8:* Use a 20-by-15-yard playing area with a 6-yard-wide goal. Play for 5 minutes or until 5 points are scored.
- *U10-U14:* Use a 30-by-15-yard playing area with an 8-yard-wide goal. Defensive team utilizes a goalkeeper as one of its 3 players. Play for 10 minutes or until 10 points are scored.

Variations

- To make the game easier for younger or less skilled players, play 4v1 in each zone.
- To make the game more challenging for older or more skilled players, allow the defender in zone 1 to move to zone 2 once the ball is in zone 2, or play 3v2 or 4v2 in each zone.

The Long Bomb

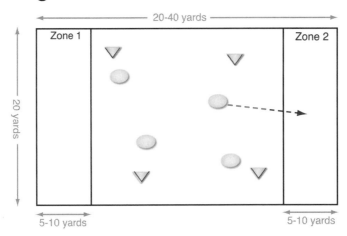

Goal

To develop and encourage long passing techniques by getting the ball to the target player

Description

Play 4v4 in a playing area with two zones, one at each end. The game begins in the center of the area, and players must pass from behind the zone line. Teams are awarded 1 point for a successful pass into a zone. After a successful pass, the game restarts with a free pass from within the zone to a player from the scoring team, and defenders must freeze while the free pass is made. If the ball goes out of play, possession changes and the game restarts with a free pass. Again, defenders must freeze while the free pass is made. Players may not make a pass to a zone directly from a restart.

- *U6:* Use a 20-by-20-yard playing area with a 5-yard zone at each end. Play for 5 minutes or until 3 to 5 points are scored.
- *U8:* Use a 30-by-20-yard playing area with a 5-yard zone at each end. Play for 10 minutes or until 5 points are scored.
- *U10-U14:* Use a 40-by-20-yard playing area with a 10-yard zone at each end. Two additional players position within the two zones and act as neutral target players who receive passes from other players. Play for 15 minutes or until 10 points are scored.

Variations

- To make the game easier for younger or less skilled players, allow players to score points by lofting or driving the ball into the zone.
- To make the game more challenging for older or more skilled players, give each player only two touches to play when she has possession, increase the field size to 60 by 30 yards, or play 5v5.

Heads Up

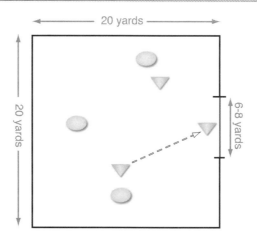

Goal

To develop heading skills

Description

Play 3v3 in a 20-square-yard area with one goal set up in the center of one sideline, as shown in the diagram. Offensive and defensive teams each consist of 3 players; the defensive team utilizes a goalkeeper as one of its 3 players. The offensive team has the ball, and the game begins in the center of the playing area. When play begins, the offensive team attempts to score as many goals as possible in 6 minutes. A kicked goal is worth 1 point. A goal scored by heading is worth 2 points. After a goal, the defensive team restarts play with a goal kick.

Teams play the game normally during minutes 1, 3, and 5. During minutes 2, 4, and 6, the coach calls, "Heads up!" to indicate a minute of heading for the team on offense. One specific player is designated the header; he will receive tosses from a teammate and attempt to head the ball into the goal past the goalkeeper as many times as possible during the allotted minute. All other players will freeze during this time. Switch teams after 6 minutes of play or when 10 points have been made.

- *U6-U10:* This activity is not appropriate for these age groups.
- *U12:* Use a 6-yard-wide goal.
- *U14:* Use an 8-yard-wide goal.

Variations

- To make the game easier for younger or less skilled players, eliminate the goalkeeper during the heading sessions.
- To make the game more challenging for older or more skilled players, play with an even number of field players.

Strike Force

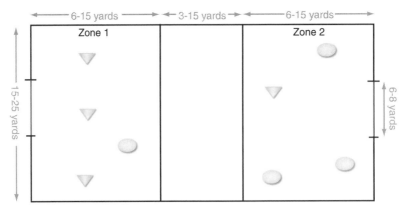

Goal

To develop shooting ability

Description

Players position in a playing area as shown in the diagram, with one goal set up at each end. Set up two zones, one at each end of the playing area, with a neutral zone in between. Players position as shown, with only one defensive player in zone 1; others are in zone 2. Play starts in zone 1. The goalkeeper (at U10-14 levels) distributes the ball to one of his team's players, or the coach throws in the ball to a specific player to begin the game. That player dribbles or passes in an effort to get the ball into the neutral zone.

All players stay in their zones except the attacker with the ball, who can move into the neutral zone to shoot. Defenders in zone 2 attempt to intercept the shot. The one attacker positioned in zone 2 works to steal the ball back and shoot it. The attacker in zone 2 can also attempt to shoot rebounds or deflections, whenever his team shoots from the neutral zone.

- *U6:* Play 3v3 in a 20-by-15-yard playing area with two 6-yard-wide goals. End zones are 6 yards wide and the neutral zone is 3 yards wide. Use no goalkeepers; the coach starts and restarts play. Play to 3 points.
- *U8:* Play 4v4 in a 20-by-25-yard playing area with two 6-yard-wide goals; end zones are 10 yards wide and the neutral zone is 5 yards wide. Use no goalkeepers; the coach starts and restarts play. Play to 5 points.
- *U10–U14:* Play 5v5 in a 45-by-25-yard playing area with two 8-yard-wide goals. Both the end zones and the neutral zone are 15 yards wide. The goalkeeper starts and restarts play; play to 7 points.

Variations

- To make the game easier for younger or less skilled players, defenders cannot intercept shots.
- To make the game harder, remove the neutral zone, create a halfway line, and restrict teams to shooting from their own halves.

Shooting Stars

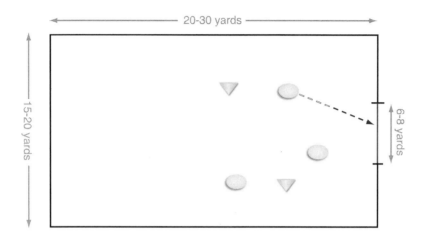

Goal

To develop shooting ability

Description

Players position in a playing area as shown in the diagram, with a goal set up at one end. Play begins with a kick-in from the goal line opposite the goal. Award 1 point for each shot attempted and 2 points for each goal. Play is restarted with a kick-in or throw-in.

- *U6:* Play 1v2 in a 20-by-15-yard playing area with a 6-yard-wide goal. Use no goalkeeper; restart play with a kick-in. Play for 3 minutes or until 3 points are scored.
- *U8:* Play 2v3 in a 20-by-15-yard playing area with a 6-yard-wide goal. Use no goalkeeper; restart play with a throw-in. Play for 5 minutes or until 4 points are scored.
- *U10–U14:* Play 3v4 in a 30-by-20-yard playing area with an 8-yard-wide goal. Utilize the goalkeeper as one of the defensive players and restart play with a throw-in. Play for 10 minutes or until 6 points are scored.

Variations

- To make the game easier for younger or less skilled players, play 5v3.
- To increase the challenge for older or more skilled players, play 2v4 or 3v5.

Hot Potato

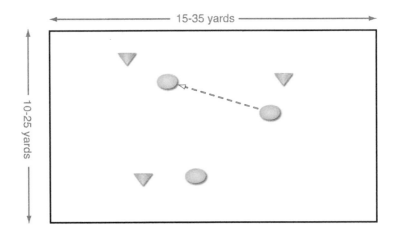

Goal

To develop receiving with the foot, thigh, or chest

Description

Players position in a playing area as shown in the diagram. Play begins with a drop ball. The focus is on controlling the ball; there are no goals to shoot at. Award 1 point for every pass received and controlled by the foot and 2 points for every pass received and controlled by the thigh or chest. Any ball that goes out of bounds is put back into play with a throw-in.

- *U6:* Play 1v1 up to 3v3 in a 15-by-10-yard playing area. Focus on ground balls.
- *U8:* Play 2v2 up to 3v3 in a 20-by-15-yard playing area. Focus primarily on ground balls, with occasional balls in the air.
- *U10-U14:* Play 3v3 in a 35-by-25-yard playing area. Focus on both ground balls and balls in the air.

Variations

- To make the game easier for younger or less skilled players, play 3v1 or 4v2 or increase the playing area to 40 by 30 yards.
- To make the game more challenging for older or more skilled players, play 2v3 or 3v4 or decrease the playing area to 30 by 20 yards.

Friend or Foe

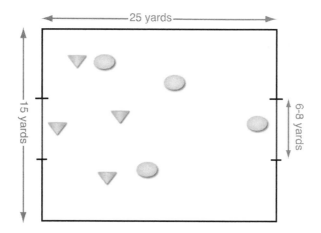

Goal

To practice the wall pass

Description

Play 4v4 in an area 25 yards long by 15 yards wide, with a goal set up at each end as shown in the diagram. Award 3 points for a successful wall pass, 2 points for an unsuccessful wall pass, and 1 point for a goal. The wall pass does not have to result in a goal to be successful—it just has to advance the ball downfield with the offense in control.

- *U6:* The activity is inappropriate for this age group.
- *U8:* Use 6-yard-wide goals and no goalkeepers.
- *U10-U14:* Use 8-yard-wide goals and utilize goalkeepers as one of the 4 players for each team.

Variations

- To make the game easier for younger or less skilled players, play 5v3, 4v2, or 3v1.
- To make the game more challenging for older or more skilled players, play 2v3 or 3v4.

Corner Kicking

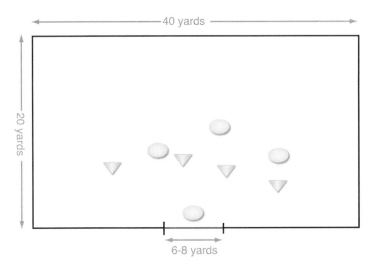

Goal

To attack and defend at corner kicks

Description

Play 4v4 in a playing area 20 yards wide by 40 yards long, with a goal set up along the length of the area on one side as shown in the diagram. Each team consists of 4 players. The offensive team gets four corner kicks (one for each player), attempting to score on each kick. Award 2 points for a goal scored directly off a corner kick and 1 point for a goal scored before the defense can control the ball. To focus on defense, you may give points only to the defense—award 1 point for not allowing a score on a corner kick. After each player has made a kick, switch teams and repeat the sequence of kicks.

- *U6:* The activity is inappropriate for this age group.
- *U8:* Use a 6-yard-wide goal and no goalkeepers.
- *U10-U14:* Use an 8-yard-wide goal and utilize a goalkeeper as one of the offensive players.

Variations

- To make the game easier for younger or less skilled players, play 5v3 or 4v2 or don't allow the defense to touch the ball first, even if they are able to do so.
- To make the game more challenging for older or more skilled players, play 4v5 or 3v5 or award points only for direct scoring from corner kicks.

Monkey on Their Backs

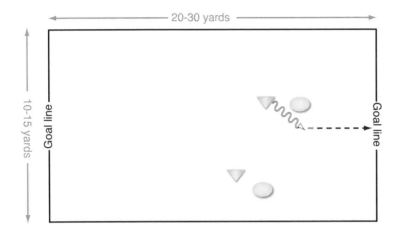

Goal

To develop marking skills

Description

Play 2v2 or 3v3 in a playing area as shown in the diagram. Each team has an end line to defend; the two end lines act as goals for the purpose of this game. Play begins in the middle of the playing area with a drop ball. Players must stay between the attacker with the ball and the defender's goal. Only the defense can earn points. Award 1 point when an attacker cannot advance the ball past her defender, either by passing or dribbling (award the point when the attacker is forced to pass back to a teammate) and 2 points if a defender intercepts or otherwise takes away the ball. When the ball goes out of bounds, play is restarted with either a kick-in or throw-in. Play to 5 points and then switch ends.

- *U6:* Use a 20-by-10-yard playing area. Play is restarted with a kick-in.
- *U8-U14:* Use a 30-by-15-yard playing area. Play is restarted with a throw-in.

Variations

- To make the game easier for younger or less skilled players, allow the offensive team more time by permitting the defense to pressure only in their half of the field. Or shorten the number of yards needed to score points by decreasing the size of the playing area.
- To make the game more challenging for more skilled players, allow the offensive team less time by permitting the defensive team to pressure full field. Or lengthen the number of yards needed to score points by increasing the size of the playing area.

The Duel

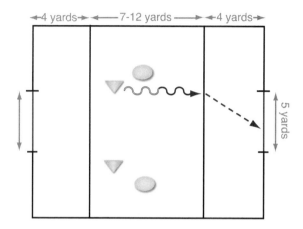

Goal

To develop tackling techniques

Description

Players position in a playing area with two 5-yard-wide goals and a 4-yard-long shooting zone set up at each end, as shown in the diagram. Play begins at midfield, and the 2 defenders try to tackle the ball while the 2 offensive players try to move the ball down the field. Once inside the 4-yard shooting zone, the offensive players can shoot on goal. If a goal is scored, the ball goes to the opposing team and play restarts with a kick-in or throw-in at its own end line. Award 2 points for any ball that is tackled and 1 point if the ball leaves the field and is awarded to the defensive team.

- *U6:* Play 1v1 in a 15-by-10-yard playing area. Play is restarted with a kick-in.
- *U8-U14:* Play 2v2 in a 20-by-15-yard playing area. Play is restarted with a throw-in.

Variations

- To make the game easier for younger or less skilled players, reduce the length of the field or play 2v3.
- To make the game more challenging for older or more skilled players, create a dividing line halfway down the field and require the defender to tackle in the opponent's half of the field only. Or create a dividing line halfway down the field, allow the attacker to pass back to a teammate to relieve pressure from the defender, and require the defender to stay at the halfway line until the attacker gets the ball back from the teammate.

Crunch Time

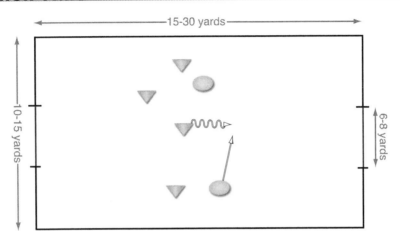

Goal

To develop block-tackling and poke-tackling techniques

Description

Players position in a playing area with a goal set up at each end, as shown in the diagram. The attacking team starts play with a kickoff. Award 1 point for each block or poke tackle made by the defense. After the defense makes a tackle, the ball is returned to the offense.

- *U6:* Play 1v1 in a 15-by-10-yard playing area with a 6-yard-wide goal; 5-minute playing time.
- *U8-U14:* Play 2v4 or 3v5 (or other lopsided configuration with more players on the defensive side) in a 30-by-15-yard playing area with an 8-yard-wide goal; 10-minute playing time.

Variations

- To make the game easier for younger or less skilled players, decrease the size of the field or add a defender.
- To make the game more challenging for older or more skilled players, increase the size of the field or add another offensive player.

Narrow Enough

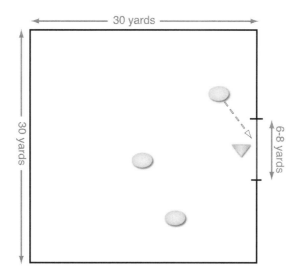

Goal

To develop the goalkeeper's ability to narrow the shooting angle

Description

Play 3v1 in a 30-square-yard area with a goal set up at one end, as shown in the diagram. The offensive team consists of 3 players and defensive team consists of 1 goalkeeper. The 3 offensive players pass among each other, attempting to score. The object is to try to shoot from the side, forcing the goalkeeper to narrow the angle to stop the shot. Award the offense 1 point for a goal scored head-on and 2 points for a goal scored from either side. Award the goalkeeper 1 point for every shot stopped. After shots are completed, rotate goalies.

- *U6 and U8:* The activity is inappropriate for these age groups.
- *U10:* Use a 6-yard-wide goal; 5 shots on goal or a 5- to 10-minute playing time.
- *U12-U14:* Use an 8-yard-wide goal; 7 shots on goal or a 10- to 15-minute playing time.

Variations

- To make the game easier for younger or less skilled players, call out the side for the shot to come from, increase the shooting distance, or use a smaller goal.
- To make the game more challenging for older or more skilled players, reduce the shooting distance, use a bigger goal, or add a player who tries to score goals from rebounds if the goalkeeper fails to deal with the shot effectively.

Keeper Wars

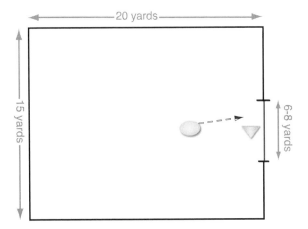

Goal

To develop and encourage the basic diving technique for goalkeepers

Description

Play 1v1 in a 20-by-15-yard playing area with a 5-foot-high goal set up at one end, as shown in the diagram. One player positions in the goal and acts as a goalkeeper, and the other player shoots at the goal. To start, the goalkeeper gets five tries to dive and save using proper technique (this game can also be adapted to focus on goalkeepers gathering air balls without diving for them). Award 1 point for each successful dive and save.

- *U6 and U8:* The activity is inappropriate for these age groups.
- *U10:* Use a 6-yard-wide goal; each player attempts to save 15 shots (15 is a perfect score).
- *U12 and U14:* Use an 8-yard-wide goal; each player attempts to save 20 shots (20 is a perfect score).

Variations

- To make the game easier for younger or less skilled players, reduce the width of the goal or require longer shots.
- To make the game more challenging for older or more skilled players, increase the width of the goal or add a player who tries to score goals from rebounds if the goalkeeper fails to deal with the shot effectively.

Bowling Balls

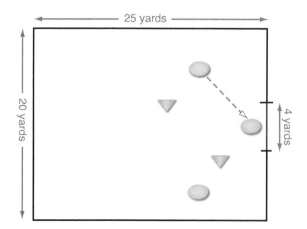

Goal

To develop the ability to distribute the ball by bowling it

Description

Play 2v3 in a 25-by-20-yard playing area with a 4-yard-wide goal set up at one end, as shown in the diagram. Teams consist of 3 players each. The 2 offensive players attack the goal. When a shot is saved, either the goalkeeper or the player who made the save bowls the ball to a teammate. Award 1 point for each ball successfully bowled (one that is controlled by one of the keeper's teammates).

- *U6 and U8:* Play 3v3, and any player who catches the ball while stopping a shot on goal is then the goalkeeper and gets to bowl the ball out.
- *U10–U14:* Play 2v3 and utilize a goalkeeper as one of the offensive players, rotating goalkeepers after three attempts at bowling the ball.

Variations

- To make the game easier for younger or less skilled players, play 1v3 or 2v4.
- To make the game more challenging for older or more skilled players, play 4v5.

On the Money

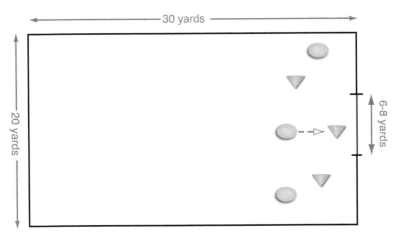

30 yards

20 yards

6-8 yards

Goal

To develop the ability to distribute the ball by throwing it

Description

Play 3v3 in a 30-by-20-yard playing area with a goal set up at one end, as shown in the diagram. The offensive team is awarded 1 point for each goal they score and for each distributed ball that they can gain possession of before the distributor's teammates do. The defense is awarded 1 point each time a player successfully distributes the ball by throwing it to a teammate who can control the ball. Once the ball is distributed, begin play again with the ball going back to the offense.

- *U6 and U8:* Use a 6-yard-wide goal. Any player who catches the ball while stopping a shot on goal is then the goalkeeper and gets to throw the ball out; 5-minute playing time.
- *U10-U14:* Use an 8-yard-wide goal and utilize a goalkeeper as one of the players on one of the teams; 10-minute playing time.

Variations

- To make the game easier for younger or less skilled players, play 2v3 or 2v4.
- To make the game more challenging for older or more skilled players, add a point for a distribution that is successfully received and controlled beyond 15 yards for younger players and beyond 20 yards for older players.

Over the Top

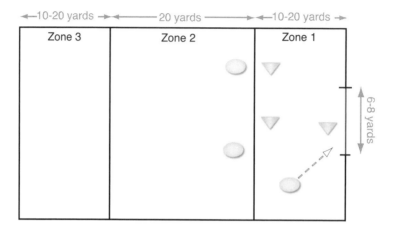

Goal

To develop the ability to distribute the ball by punting it

Description

Play 3v3 in a playing area divided into zones, with a goal set up at one end as shown in the diagram. The offensive team consists of 3 players, and the defensive team consists of 3 players, the latter utilizing a goalkeeper as one of its players. The offensive team attacks the goal and the defensive team defends it. The defense is awarded points for shots that the keeper stops and successfully distributes by punting the ball: 1 point if the ball lands within zone 2 (the middle 20 yards), 2 points if the ball lands within zone 3 (the farthest 20 yards), and 1 additional point for any punt that is controlled by one of the keeper's teammates. After each defensive player has had three chances to punt, switch teams.

- *U6 and U8:* The activity is inappropriate for these age groups.
- *U10:* Play in a 40-by-20-yard playing area with 10-yard zones; use a 6-yard-wide goal.
- *U12-U14:* Play in a 60-by-20-yard playing area with 20-yard zones; use an 8-yard-wide goal.

Variations

- To make the game easier for younger or less skilled players, reduce the length of the field or instruct the offense to kick the ball easily to the keeper to begin play and not to try to score a goal.
- To make the game more challenging for older or more skilled players, give keepers a point for catching the ball cleanly or increase the length of the field.

What's the Scoop

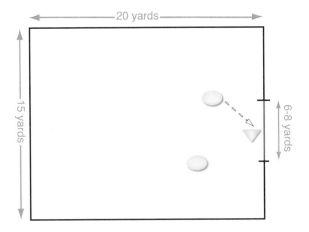

Goal

To develop the ability to gather ground balls

Description

Play 2v1 in a 20-by-15-yard playing area with a goal set up at one end, as shown in the diagram. The 2 attackers try to score on the goalkeeper. The attackers take five shots on goal, passing between themselves and trying to get the best shot possible. The keeper is awarded 2 points for a clean scoop (one in which he cleanly gathers the ball) and 1 point for any other type of save. The goalkeeper receives no points if a goal is scored. To restart play, the goalkeeper tosses the ball back to the attackers. After every five chances to defend the goal, rotate players so that everyone has a chance to play keeper.

- *U6 and U8:* The activity is inappropriate for these age groups.
- *U10:* Use a 6-yard-wide goal.
- *U12 and U14:* Use an 8-yard-wide goal.

Variations

- To make the game easier for younger or less skilled players, increase the shot length or decrease the speed of the shots.
- To make the game more challenging for older or more skilled players, have players shoot to the corners or increase the speed of the shots.

About the Author

Coaching Youth Soccer was written by the American Sport Education Program (ASEP) in conjunction with Sam Snow, director of coaching education for US Youth Soccer. ASEP has been developing and delivering coaching education courses since 1981. As the nation's leading coaching education program, ASEP works with national, state, and local youth sport organizations to develop educational programs for coaches, officials, administrators, and parents. These programs incorporate ASEP's philosophy of "Athletes first, Winning second."

For more coaching information go to USYouthSoccer.org to register or call...

1.800.4.SOCCER

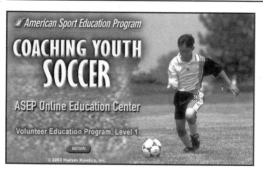

Collins

Atlas of
Military
History

Collins

Atlas of Military History